MYLNE'S COURT

*Three hundred years of
Lawnmarket heritage*

ROBERT MYLNE
from a painting by Roderick Chalmers.

Frontispiece

MYLNE'S COURT

Three hundred years of
Lawnmarket heritage

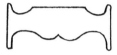

ROY M. PINKERTON and WILLIAM J. WINDRAM

1983

Published by University of Edinburgh Information Office
Old College, South Bridge, Edinburgh

ISBN 0 902511 20 3

Printed and bound by Clark Constable (1982) Ltd, Edinburgh

CONTENTS

PLATES

Plate 2 is reproduced here by courtesy of the National Galleries of Scotland, plate 4 by courtesy of Edinburgh City Libraries, and plates 3, 5, 6, 11, and 13 by courtesy of the University of Edinburgh. Plates 1 and 12 are reproduced from J. Grant, *Old and New Edinburgh* (London 1880-3) and *Frontispiece* from R. S. Mylne, *The Master Masons to the Crown of Scotland* (Edinburgh 1893). Plates 7, 8, 9, and 10 are from photographs taken by R. M. Pinkerton.

The design and execution of the front cover, showing the Lawnmarket frontage of Mylne's Court today, is the work of Andrew M. Pinkerton, to whom grateful thanks are due.

INTRODUCTION

Stand in Edinburgh's Princes Street and look up to one of the noblest townscapes any European city can offer: the Mound, New College, Ramsay Garden, and the towers and battlements of Edinburgh Castle soaring above them all. Or stand on the ramparts of the Castle itself and follow the line of the Royal Mile, threading its way down between the tall lands of the Old Town, cradle of so much of Scotland's history. Playing its part in each of these scenes is the building which is the subject of much of this book: Mylne's Court. Its south block, in the Lawnmarket, is itself part of the Royal Mile, while the crow-stepped gables of its north block peep out from behind the towers of New College, their windows affording a glimpse of Princes Street far below.

Mylne's Court was built in 1690, its open courtyard a completely new concept in contemporary Scottish town-planning; restored in the 1960s, it now functions as a hall of residence for students at the University of Edinburgh. In the intervening years, its history has been typical of much of the Royal Mile: once the proud home of a cross-section of the capital's citizens, its social standing declined as the New Town superseded the Old, and eighteenth-century grandeur gave way to nineteenth-century decline and twentieth-century dilapidation.

It is a story that deserves to be told, and told perhaps by more expert hands than ours: no doubt the town-planner could assess Mylne's Court's original significance more fully, the sociologist expound at greater length its contribution to the everyday life of the city, the architect discuss in finer detail the complexities of its recent restoration. The following pages simply look back over the last three hundred years and attempt to give a general picture of the building, its inhabitants, and their lives; nearby properties now associated with Mylne's Court are dealt with in the final two chapters; and an epilogue comments on life today in this part of the Old Town.

ACKNOWLEDGEMENTS

Our self-imposed task of reviewing the history of Mylne's Court, carried out over several years in such odd moments as could be spared from lives busy with teaching and learning, has been considerably lightened by the encouragement of a number of friends, whose regular enquiries after the progress of our work gave us sufficient incentive to bring it to completion.

Our warm thanks are due to those who have helped materially, either by contributing information or by directing us to its source: Dr Philip Boardman, Very Rev. Professor John McIntyre, Miss Marjorie Matheson, Lesley Millar, Rev. Fraser Stewart, Mr Richard Telfer, and Miss Elma Webster. The late Sir James Monteith Grant, Lord Lyon King of Arms, and Dr Walter H. Makey, Archivist to the City of Edinburgh, responded generously to our pleas for advice. Several families who had lived in Mylne's Court before it was taken over by the University were happy to talk about their time there, and to Mrs Evelyn Anderson and Mr William Brydon in particular we are grateful for giving us a clear picture of what their lives in the building were like.

Any work of this kind owes an incalculable amount to the staff of libraries and similar institutions. Throughout our investigations, we have met with nothing but courtesy and efficiency, and we now gladly acknowledge our very real debt to the staffs of New College Library; the Special Collections Department, Edinburgh University Library; the Buildings Office, University of Edinburgh; the Archives and Records Centre, University of Strathclyde; the Edinburgh Room, Edinburgh Central Public Library; the Royal Commission on the Ancient and Historical Monuments of Scotland; and the Print Room, National Gallery of Scotland.

Much of the information on the Mylne family in chapter 2 is taken from Rev. R. S. Mylne's important study *The Master Masons to the Crown of Scotland*. Miss Minnie Nicol, a direct descendant of Robert Mylne, presented to Mylne's Court in 1974 a copy of this rare work; this generous gesture was the direct impetus for our researches. Information relating to census returns in chapter 6 is derived from records in the custody of the Registrar General for Scotland, and is published with his permission.

For reading the text and for suggesting a number of improvements, our warm thanks go to Ronald Knox (who also allowed us to borrow, on extended loan, valuable items from his library), to Ron Smith, and in particular to Andrew Fraser, whose expert knowledge of old Edinburgh saved us from many a mistake. Our thanks go also to Doris Williamson, who with commendable skill and accuracy reduced the untidiness of our manuscript to the perfection of typescript (and corrected at least one historical error in the process).

The publication of our work would not have been possible without the help and encouragement of several people within the University of Edinburgh, and to them we express our most sincere appreciation: Professor Neil MacCormick, Chairman of the Accommodation Committee; Dr Philip Ross and Dr Francis Barnes, Senior Wardens; and Ray Footman, Information Officer.

Non opis est nostrae dignas persoluere grates: our story is told, and for such blemishes as it may have we can only crave the reader's indulgence. One final acknowledgement remains: to Mylne's Court itself. To have lived there for several years, one of us as its warden and the other as a student resident, was an enriching experience, and we dedicate this result of our researches to all those, through the centuries, who have found in it a home and who have helped to create both its past and its present.

R.M.P.
W.J.W.
Edinburgh, 1983

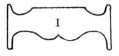

"DEVIOUS, VARIED, AND TALL":
the Lawnmarket and Robert Mylne

Above the entranceway of the passage leading from the Lawn-market to Mylne's Court is an ornamental pediment bearing the date 1690. This was the year in which the construction of the Court was begun, but to use it as a starting-point in any account of the building's history is to omit one of the most important parts of the story. In one sense that story begins far back in the mists of time, when the rocks of Scotland were being shaped into their present form by the great primeval forces of nature. The resulting geological formation determined to a large extent the growth of the Old Town of Edinburgh, and it is in the replacement of the early buildings of this Old Town with the open courtyards of the late seventeenth century that the significance of Mylne's Court lies.

The Old Town of Edinburgh is a classic example of what geologists call a 'crag and tail'. The 'crag' is the rock on which the Castle now stands, and was formed by solidified and unerupted lava plugging one of the vents of the Arthur's Seat volcano. Millions of years later, as the ice-sheets of the Pleistocene glaciers moved eastwards across the Central Scottish plain, their progress was barred by this massive plug of basalt: as the ice split into two to circumvent it, deep gorges were gouged out on each side of the Castle rock, forming what is now the site of Princes Street Gardens on the north and the line of the Grassmarket and the Cowgate on the south. Before the two prongs of the ice-sheet could merge again, a thin 'tail' of ground was left in the immediate lee of the Castle rock, unaffected by the passage of the ice. On this narrow, sloping ridge, almost a mile long, between the Castle and David I's twelfth-century Abbey of Holyrood, there sprang up the earliest dwellings of what is now Scotland's capital, the ancient royalty of the burgh of Edinburgh spreading downwards from the Castle and the burgh of the Canongate climbing upwards from Holyrood, the two eventually meeting to form the Royal Mile.

By the early seventeenth century, Edinburgh had grown considerably and the Royal Mile was now the principal thoroughfare of a busy and flourishing community. In the Canongate the street was narrow, but west of St Giles it widened for several hundred yards to provide sufficient space for the booths and stalls of a street market, such widening being a characteristic feature of early Scottish town development still to be seen elsewhere throughout the country. The section of the Royal Mile between St Giles and Castlehill is still known as the Lawnmarket, the first element of the name indicating either that lawn merchants sold linen and other kinds of cloth in the market here or, if 'Lawnmarket' is to be understood as a corruption of 'Landmarket', that this was where the goods from the land, i.e. country produce, were sold. The stalls were of course only temporary erections, but at the upper limit of the market a more permanent structure occupied the middle of the street, in the shape of a Weigh House. Four such buildings in succession stood at the junction of the Lawnmarket and Castlehill: the first two were known also as Butter Trons, thus indicating the principal commodity for which they were designed, but on the completion of the more imposing third Weigh House in 1614 the Town Council stipulated that it was to be used not just for butter, cheese, and such-like country produce, but for the weighing of all merchandise over two pounds weight. It was in this building that Cromwell mounted a guard when he laid siege to Edinburgh Castle in 1650 and on his capture of the fortress the Weigh House was demolished. A replacement was built in 1660, with a cellar commodious enough to be used as a gaol on occasions, and this remained in existence until 1822. Not only had it by then served its purpose, but it was also somewhat of an obstruction to the ever-increasing flow of traffic, and the need to widen the approach to the Castle in preparation for George IV's famous visit to Edinburgh in that year was the excuse for the final disappearance of a Weigh House from the Lawnmarket. Ironically, the site of this obstruction to nineteenth-century traffic is now marked by a traffic island, enabling the much greater volume of twentieth-century traffic to negotiate the busy junction between Johnston Terrace and the Royal Mile.

Johnston Terrace and the Tolbooth Kirk were nineteenth-century innovations, and until the Lawnmarket was so radically altered by these additions it was lined on both sides by houses. Gordon of Rothiemay's city plan of 1647 provides a striking, if somewhat diagrammatic, impression of what this part of Edinburgh looked like in the mid-seventeenth century. The buildings are packed tightly together, running in long rows at right angles to the Lawnmarket down both slopes of the ridge, south to the Grassmarket, and north towards the Nor' Loch, which at that time filled the deep glacial valley below. The density of building may be gauged from the fact that between the present entry to Mylne's Court and the next surviving entry to the west, Sempill's Close, a distance of approximately eighty yards, there were the frontages of no fewer than six tenements, or 'Lands', as they were known, with five pends running between them. Gordon's plan, however, can hardly be taken at face value. The tenements were almost certainly not arranged in neat, parallel rows, the old town having developed in somewhat haphazard fashion over the centuries. If a building collapsed or burnt down — and the predominance of timber or thatch meant that the risk of fire was ever present — the empty space was immediately infilled, not in accordance with any preconceived plan, but simply in order to provide accommodation for as many people as possible: a veritable rabbit-warren of pends, wynds and alleyways thus grew up. Another reason for the town's growth in this way was that such events as the Scots defeat at Flodden in 1513, together with the threat of later English attacks such as Henry VIII's 'Rough Wooing' of 1544, had so frightened the citizens that once the Flodden Wall was completed in 1560 they tended to avail themselves of its protection and only rarely would consider dwelling outside its perimeter. A steadily increasing population confined within the walls of the medieval burgh soon produced the obvious result: the only direction in which to build more living space was upwards, and houses many storeys high began to make their appearance in the early seventeenth century. The recent commentator who characterised these buildings as "dense, tightly-packed, devious, varied, and tall"[1] perhaps provides a more realistic description than the regimentation of Gordon's plan.

3

Small wonder that housing of such a type gave rise to problems. Building standards were low, fire was a constant source of worry, and inevitably, with so many people living in such close proximity to one another, standards of hygiene were anything but adequate. To its credit, the Town Council made valiant attempts throughout the seventeenth century to improve matters, often supported by Acts of Parliament. As early as 1621, for example, Parliament ordained that no new building in Edinburgh was to be thatched, and in 1681 owners of older houses which still retained their thatch were given one year to replace it with lead, slates, or tiles. In 1674, following a disastrous fire at the head of Todrig's Wynd, the Town Council decreed that stone and not wood was to be used both in the repair of damaged buildings and in the construction of new ones, while owners of wooden buildings were to be given exemption from taxation for seventeen years if they rebuilt in stone. Later that year, more drastic measures were adopted, and it was stipulated that all new buildings with a frontage along the Royal Mile should be of equal height (restricted to five storeys by an Act of Parliament in 1698), that the upper storeys should project the same width out over the street and should be supported by pillars and arches (such as are still to be seen at Gladstone's Land in the Lawnmarket), and that entry to the buildings was to be gained not from the street, by wooden stairs encroaching upon the public way as hitherto, but from the back premises. Other improvements making for a higher standard of living in the last quarter of the seventeenth century were the introduction of a water supply and public lighting in the streets, stricter regulations concerning street cleaning, and a requirement that owners of houses fronting the street should have pavements made.

By their very nature, however, such piece-meal attempts at improvement could be merely short-term. The fundamental problem, the need for more building space, still had to be tackled, and it was eventually realised by the Town Council that the only permanent solution was to extend the boundaries of the city by bridging the valleys to the north and south of the Royal Mile, and then to build on the open spaces beyond. Accordingly, in 1688 the Lord Provost, Sir Magnus Spence, went to Whitehall and secured the necessary permission to extend the city, but the political situation prevented his plans from being carried out and it was not

4

until well on in the next century that final agreement was reached on the long-awaited proposals for development.

To some extent, however, private enterprise succeeded where officialdom was frustrated. Among Edinburgh's distinguished citizens was a man possessed not only of a vision, but of the necessary social and financial standing to enable this vision to be translated into reality. Robert Mylne, a successful architect who in 1668 had been appointed Master Mason to the King, recognised the need for less cramped housing conditions. Making use of an Act of the Scots Parliament of 1644 which authorised Town Councils to sell off ground which had become waste or ruined tenements which had not been rebuilt, he bought up property, demolished or refurbished existing buildings, and erected new ones where necessary: not rows of tall lands opening off narrow pends, but buildings grouped round a square, central courtyard. With such an arrangement there was not merely light and fresh air, but a spaciousness which made for a pleasanter and a healthier life; the children had somewhere to play; and of course a courtyard was a much more congenial place to sit and gossip in than the narrow, twisting, smelly stairs of the old tenements: the whole concept was as revolutionary in its own day as the skyscrapers of some two and a half centuries later. Two such courtyards were built by Mylne, both on the north side of the Royal Mile: Mylne's Square opposite the Tron Kirk and Mylne's Court beside the Weigh House. The enthusiasm with which they were greeted led other builders to follow in Mylne's footsteps, and several other courts soon appeared on both sides of the street, the best surviving example being James Court, built by James Brownhill in the 1720s.

Mylne's Square was built between 1684 and 1688, "ane fabrick the front quherof of polished aisler* work of competent thickness, and the back work nixt to the court of good rich meassone work of tuo fute and half foots breadth".[2] Six, and in some places seven, storeys high, the buildings had an imposing appearance, with some attractive corbelling, handsome doorways, and an arched pend leading from the High Street. In Mylne's words, he hoped that the square "might not only prove to the decorment of the good Town but to the great convenience and accommodation of his Majesty's

---

* *aisler*: ashlar, i.e. constructed of blocks of square-hewn stone

lieges therein and resorting thereto".[3] The scheme proved popular, and such of his Majesty's lieges as were successful in obtaining accommodation therein were of a somewhat superior quality, including a number of advocates, a Senator of the College of Justice, the Earl of Northesk, and Lady Airdry, widow of a Lieutenant-Governor of Edinburgh Castle: no wonder that a mere cobbler who attempted to set up his stall within the square was summarily ejected.

Within twenty years of its completion, Mylne's Square was the scene of three important events in Scottish history. In 1695, the newly founded Bank of Scotland rented premises in the square and established there its first temporary office, before moving the following year to more permanent accommodation in Parliament Close. Thereafter, the same flat was rented by 'The Company of Scotland', the enthusiastic promoters of that ill-fated business enterprise, the Darien Expedition. Here its Directors met regularly, making their plans for the foundation of that colony which, far from increasing Scotland's prosperity, was to bring her almost to the brink of economic disaster. A few years later, in 1707, a cellar in the square was the place where the fateful Articles of Union, marking the end of Scottish independence, were signed and sealed. The Commissioners had gathered for this purpose at Moray House, but on being driven from there by an infuriated mob they took refuge in a basement shop below one of the tenements in Mylne's Square.

This first essay in spacious living unfortunately no longer exists. In 1787 the east side of the square, which projected rather inconveniently into the new North Bridge, was partially taken down and rebuilt, and the whole square was finally demolished in the 1890s to allow for the widening of the bridge, which had by then become a particularly busy traffic artery.

Mylne's Square was scarcely completed when his second, and slightly smaller, courtyard was started in the Lawnmarket. The similarity in style, in date, and in name between Mylne's Court and Mylne's Square has led to considerable confusion between them, and many a book on old Edinburgh attributes to the one what really belongs to the other. For long, Mylne's Court was regarded as somewhat inferior to its predecessor, but fate has dealt more kindly with it. It may now have only three sides instead of its

6

original four, but it has overcome several threats to its existence and has weathered decades of neglect. It now stands restored to some of its former glory as Edinburgh's earliest surviving example of domestic dwelling designed to form an open courtyard, while its student inhabitants play a vital role in ensuring that the life of the Lawnmarket still pulses with vigour and exuberance.

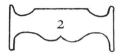

"MASTER MASONS TO A ROYAL RACE":
the Mylne family[4]

No account of architectural developments in Scotland in the sixteenth and seventeenth centuries can fail to accord a prominent place to the name of Mylne. In a quite remarkable record of public service, no fewer than seven members of the family, in an almost direct line of succession, held the office of Master Mason to the Crown of Scotland for much of the period between 1481 and 1710, serving eleven monarchs during a time in which a vast amount of building, both public and private, was carried out. A Master Mason combined the functions of a modern architect, surveyor, contractor, and clerk of works; the office of Master Mason to the Crown, which was generally conferred for life, was one of the minor offices of state which gave its incumbent general oversight of building works at all royal palaces and castles throughout Scotland, under the ultimate supervision of the King's Master of Works. The Master Mason to the Crown usually held other appointments, such as Master Mason in one of the major cities of the kingdom, and in addition frequently carried on an extensive — and lucrative — private practice. The Mylne family, of course, did not have a monopoly of this office — Thomas Franche, John Roytell, William Schaw, and William Wallace were other distinguished holders of it — but no other family left its mark so clearly on the history of Scottish building over so long a period.

The family name appears in early records as both 'Mylne' and 'Milne', and occasionally also in the form 'Mill': it is appropriate that this variation in spelling should be perpetuated today, the local authority favouring 'Milne' on its maps and street-signs, the University preferring 'Mylne'. Robert Mylne of Balfarg, who gave his name to Mylne's Court, was Master Mason to the Crown from 1668 until his death in 1710. He was the seventh and last of his name to be appointed to the position (not, be it noted, the 'seventh

Royal Master Mason', as he is often erroneously described, but simply the seventh Mylne to hold the title). To the building up of the strong family tradition to which Robert fell heir, each of his six predecessors* had made his own distinctive contribution.

The connection of the family with the crown began in the reign of James III, who in 1481 appointed John Mylne as his Master Mason. This appointment was confirmed by James IV, and was held by Mylne until his death sometime before 1513. Little is known about this first Mylne, but he would almost certainly have had some responsibility for the major works at Stirling Castle, where the imposing Gatehouse and the magnificent Great Hall were being added to the fortress, and at Linlithgow, where additions and alterations to James I's palace were being made. He does not appear, however, to have had any part in the principal piece of new building under James IV, the erection of what is now the north-west tower of the Palace of Holyroodhouse.

His son, Alexander, was an important figure in both church and state, who combined with his various other duties the office of Master Mason to James V for a brief period in the 1520s. He was primarily a churchman, successively Rector of Lundy, Canon of Dunkeld, Prebendary of Monifeith, Official of the Diocese of Dunkeld (i.e. Judge of the Bishop's Consistory Court), Dean of Angus, and from 1517, Abbot of Cambuskenneth, where he was responsible for building the chapter-house and the high altar, and for laying out two cemeteries. He was also a man of letters, who wrote a Latin history of the Bishops of Dunkeld from 1127 to 1515, and had such expertise and experience in legal matters that James V appointed him the first President of the Court of Session when that august body of "cunning and wise"[5] men was instituted in 1532; this exalted position he held with distinction until his death in 1548. The inauguration ceremony of the Court of Session is depicted in one of Edinburgh's most striking stained-glass windows, the south window of Parliament Hall, in the central panel of which Mylne is to be seen kneeling before James V to receive from him the Papal charter of institution and confirmation.

At this point the line of succession becomes a little blurred. Thomas, the third of the family to be King's Master Mason, an

* For a simplified pedigree of the Mylne family, see fig. 1.

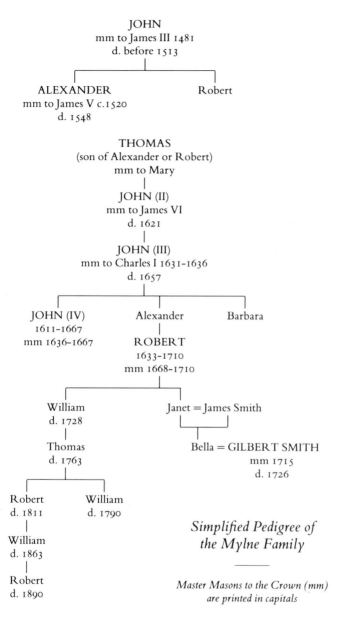

JOHN
mm to James III 1481
d. before 1513

ALEXANDER   Robert
mm to James V c.1520
      d. 1548

THOMAS
(son of Alexander or Robert)
mm to Mary

JOHN (II)
mm to James VI
      d. 1621

JOHN (III)
mm to Charles I 1631-1636
      d. 1657

JOHN (IV)   Alexander   Barbara
1611-1667
mm 1636-1667   ROBERT
                    1633-1710
                    mm 1668-1710

William   Janet = James Smith
d. 1728

Thomas   Bella = GILBERT SMITH
d. 1763   mm 1715
                          d. 1726

Robert   William
d. 1811   d. 1790

William   *Simplified Pedigree of*
d. 1863   *the Mylne Family*

Robert
d. 1890   *Master Masons to the Crown (mm)*
                   are printed in capitals

FIGURE I

office which he apparently held at some stage between 1561 and
1579, is described as the son of the aforementioned Alexander in
the pedigree of Robert Mylne of Balfarg recorded in the Lyon
Register. Other authorities make him Alexander's nephew, son of
his brother Robert, a Burgess of Dundee and its Provost in 1547.
Thomas is a shadowy figure, and he probably had little to do in any
case: hardly any public building was being carried out in the 1560s
and 1570s, in the aftermath of the Reformation and with the
virtual collapse of civil government in the country following upon
the deposition of Mary and during the minority of James VI.

Thomas's son, John (II), was a more substantial figure. Master
Mason to James VI, his name appears frequently in Dundee records
in the 1580s and the 1590s. Early in the following decade he moved
to Perth, where he was engaged in building a much-needed new
bridge across the Tay. The bridge was completed in 1616 and with
its line of long, low arches was regarded as Mylne's greatest work.
Unfortunately, however, it had been built too low to withstand
flood water, and it did not survive him long: Mylne died early in
1621, and on 14 October of that year the bridge was washed away
during a tremendous storm. He is buried in Greyfriars burial
ground, Perth, where his gravestone proclaimed that

> This stone entombs the dust of famous Mill
> Renowned chiefly in his time for skill;
> In architecture his learned art did lay
> The spatious arches of the Bridge of Tay,
> Which was demolish'd by a mighty spate:
> So was his fabrick by the course of fate;

not completely demolished, however, for although

> Seven foot of ground, clay floor, clay wall,
> Serve both for chamber now and hall
> To Master Mill, whose squirbuily* braine
> Could ten Escurialls well containe
> Whill he breath'd lyfe, yet in his sonne
> And sonn's sone he lives two for one
> Who to advance Mill's art and fame
> Make stocks and stones speak out his name.

* *squirbuily*: capacious

12

During the building of the Perth Bridge, he had been assisted by his son John (III), who on 17 December 1631 was created by Charles I "our Principall Maister Maissoun within our castell of Edinbrugh and all vtheris our castellis palaces strenthis forthis or ony vther our workis quhair he salbe resident for the tyme at work or quhairwith he salbe imployit be our saidis maisteris of work". As payment, in addition to "all priviledges liberties friedomes and commodities pertening thairto", Mylne was to receive "the soume of Ten pundis money of this our said realme of Scotland" monthly, together with "ane honest stand of cloathing yeirlie". As early as 1617, this third John had been connected with commissions involving the royal family, when he came to Edinburgh to complete the construction of the statue of James VI, erected at the Netherbow Port in preparation for the welcome ceremony held there on the occasion of James' first visit to Scotland since his departure for England in 1603. In the next few years, John Mylne was much involved with minor works throughout Scotland, in 1618 at Dundee, in 1619 at Falkland, in 1622 at Aberdeen, and in 1629 at Drummond Castle. In that year he was employed by Charles I to make a new 'water-pond' at Holyroodhouse, the satisfactory completion of which must have contributed to his appointment as Master Mason to the Crown in 1631. His principal tasks in that office were the execution of the splendid sundial in the north garden of the Palace of Holyroodhouse, with its polyhedral head and its twenty-nine dials, and the alterations at St Giles consequent upon Charles I's establishment of it as the cathedral church of the new Bishopric of Edinburgh. Edinburgh did not agree with him, however, and despite the fact that Charles' grant had been "during all the dayis of his lyftyme" he resigned his royal appointment in 1636 and retired to Dundee, where he busied himself with various private works until his death in 1657.

Three of his children, Barbara, Alexander, and another John (IV), made names for themselves. Barbara was from time to time accused of witchcraft, the most notorious occasion being in July 1661, when, as a minute of the Edinburgh Town Council records, she was seen by one Janet Allen, herself later burnt as a witch, when she came in "by the Water Gate in the likeness of a catt, and did change her garment under her awen staire, and went into her house".[6] Her two brothers followed more respectable professions, continuing in different ways the family tradition. The younger one, Alexander, was particularly skilled in the embellishment of buildings with small-scale sculptures, one of his most noteworthy achievements being the Royal Arms which he executed for the frontage of Parliament House. When this frontage was renewed in 1808, the sculptures were considered too good to be thrown away, and were rescued by Lord President Dundas for use at his house at Arniston. Alexander died of the plague in 1643, and was buried in the Abbey of Holyrood, where his gravestone (now fixed to the outer wall of the building in the private gardens of the Palace) pays lavish tribute to his skill in the lines:

> Siste, hospes; clarus jacet hoc sub marmore Milnus
> Dignus qui Pharius conderet ossa labor;
> Quod vel in aere Myron fudit vel pinxit Appelles,
> Artifici hoc potuit hic lapicida manu.

> Stay, passenger; here famous Milne doth rest,
> Worthy to be in Aegypt's marble drest:
> What Myron or Appelles could have done
> In Brasse or Paintry, hee could that in Stone.

Alexander's elder brother, John (IV), held more closely to the traditions of the family and succeeded his father as royal Master Mason in 1636, the sixth of the family to hold the office. Born in 1611, and holding his royal appointment from 1636 until his death on Christmas Eve 1667, he led a life of distinguished public service. He was Master Mason to the city of Edinburgh, where he was also a Burgess and a member of the Town Council; in 1646 he was appointed by Charles I "Captane and Maister of all Warkmen of Workis and Pioneris of our houses fortis strenthis and palices within our kingdome of Scotland and ... Principall Maister Gunner within our castle of Edinburgh and also within all wther castellis strenthis and fortressis within our said kingdome of Scotland"; he was a member of the Committee of Estates in 1648 and 1651; he was one of the twenty-one Commissioners from Scotland who went to the English Parliament in 1652 (they went to discuss the formation of a Treaty of Union with England, but nine months later "they returned having done litell or nothing"); he represented Edinburgh at the Convention of Royal Burghs from 1655 to 1659; and he was a Commissioner from the city of Edinburgh to the Scots Parliament in 1662 and again in 1668.

Professionally, his building activity included the supervision of the Tron Church in Edinburgh (completed in 1647), the restoration of portions of St Giles, the completion of Heriot's Hospital, and the construction of the fortifications of Leith. His expertise was in demand in other parts of Scotland: he was, for example, commissioned by the Presbytery of Jedburgh to report on "the decayed state of the Abbey church"; he duly reported it to be in such a dilapidated condition "that it is a wonder how either the minister dar be bold to preay or the people to heer", and in recognition of his services he was enrolled as a Freeman of the Burgh of Jedburgh. He was associated also with the University of Edinburgh: in 1647, he made additions to the buildings of the 'Tounis College', as it was then known, and in 1656 he supervised further extensions, including a house for the Professor of Divinity and "six chambers for the students". He is buried in Greyfriars churchyard, where an ornate monument to his memory stands against its east wall, to the south of the main gate, praising him in typically fulsome terms:

> Great artisan, grave senator, John Milne,
> Renowned for learning, prudence, parts, and skill,
> Who in his life Vitruvius' art had shown
> Adorning other monuments: his own
> Can have no other beauty than his name,
> His memory, and everlasting fame . . .

and reminding the inevitable passer-by of the family's proud record:

> Reader, John Milne, who maketh the fourth John
> And by descent from father unto son
> Sixth Master Mason to a royal race
> Of seven successive kings, sleeps in this place.

Such was the family tradition inherited by the builder of Mylne's Court. Robert Mylne was born in 1633, the eldest son of Alexander the sculptor. In 1668, on 28 February, he was appointed Master Mason to the Crown in succession to his uncle John, thus becoming the seventh Mylne to hold the post; and he remained in that office from then until his death in 1710, forty-two years and four reigns later. When he was buried in his uncle's grave in Greyfriars his inscription stated that he

> had more skill
> In mason craft himself alone
> Than most his brethren joined in one

and singled out as worthy of especial mention the fact that "during an active life of honest fame [he] builded among manie extensive works Mylne's Court, Mylne's Square, and The Abbie of Halierud House". Among his "manie extensive works" were the new Cross of Perth, Wood's Hospital at Largo, Leslie House (a new seat for the Earl of Rothes), seven additional wells or cisterns to improve Edinburgh's water supply, a single-arched bridge over the Clyde at Romellweill Crags, a few miles south of Roberton, and the Mylne Battery at Edinburgh Castle, a list which shows the diversity of his skill if nothing else. Private housing also attracted him: in addition to the revolutionary creations of Mylne's Square and Mylne's Court, he built tenements close to the harbour at Leith for his own use. It was the Palace of Holyroodhouse, however, which claimed most of his time and energy: this is not the place to recount the major works of reconstruction undertaken by Charles II and supervised by Mylne, but it is to him more than to any other single person that Holyroodhouse owes its present appearance. Here, too, Mylne left his mark in a literal sense, for his initials can still be traced on a pillar at the north west corner of the courtyard.

In 1661 Mylne married Elisabeth Meikle of Cramond, and at his death, according to the Greyfriars monument, left "eight sonnes and six daughters all placed in the world with credit to himself". A prominent Edinburgh citizen whose name appears regularly in the Burgh records of the time, he was elected Deacon of the Masons in 1674, and held that office on several subsequent occasions, serving also for a spell as a representative Deacon on the Town Council. He owned the estate of Balfarg, or Balfargie, in Fife, and in 1672 matriculated arms at the Lyon Office, choosing as the principal device on his shield a cross moline: the *crux molendinarium* or *ferrum molendinarium* was an iron instrument fixed in the lower mill-stone to guide the upper one as it moved, and so this type of cross was particularly appropriate for those with the surname Mill, Miller,

Milne, etc. According to the entry in the Lyon Register, the crest was "Apelles' head couped at the shoulders", Apelles being the celebrated painter of Alexander the Great whose skill in "Paintry" was recalled in Mylne's father's epitaph. Curiously, family tradition among the Mylnes identifies the crest as "Pallas' head", Pallas, or Minerva, being the goddess of wisdom: this identification is supported by a list of several of her attributes, including the fact that "the art of building, especially castles, was Minerva's invention and therefore she was believed to preside over them".[7] Minerva, however, is not particularly associated in the Classical world with building, and it is more likely that at some stage the phrase "Apelles' head" became corrupted to "a Pallas' head". The motto Mylne chose was *tam arte quam Marte* ('as much by skill as by force of arms').

With his death, the connection between the name of Mylne and the office of Master Mason to the Crown came to an end, not through any diminution of the family's talents, but rather by the disappearance of the office itself. After the accession of William and Mary in 1688, the officials of the Stuart court were looked on with disfavour, and although the rights, privileges, and life interests of such people as Robert Mylne were protected, it is probable that the office meant little after that date. On the Union of the Parliaments in 1707, there was little point in retaining many of the minor offices of the Scottish crown, and when Robert Mylne's grandson-in-law, Gilbert Smith, was appointed Master Mason in 1715 the appointment was not for life, but only during George I's pleasure. This apparently did not last for long, as the office was shortly taken over by a Commission, later to become HM Office of Works, the forerunner of the present-day Department of the Environment. This Gilbert Smith's wife, Bella, was a daughter of James Smith, one of Mylne's partners who had married his daughter Janet: not only did she present James with the first eighteen of his thirty-two children, but she was also, according to her husband, "a good drawer and very clever".

Although there was no longer a royal office for them to hold, the descendants of Robert Mylne were nevertheless distinguished in their profession. His son William, William's son Thomas, and Thomas's younger son William were all notable architects, the last-named being the architect of the North Bridge in Edinburgh, finished in 1772. Thomas's elder son, Robert, who settled in London and was responsible, amongst much else, for the controversial elliptical arches of Blackfriars Bridge, is remembered in Scotland principally for his work at Inveraray Castle and in replanning the village of Inveraray; he also designed St Cecilia's Hall, one of Edinburgh University's architectural gems. The end of the line is reached with this Robert's grandson, another Robert (1817-90), an architect and surveyor based mainly in Birmingham, to whom credit is due for his discovery that the building being used as one of the powder stores at Edinburgh Castle was in reality Queen Margaret's chapel: the identification and subsequent restoration of this ancient shrine was one of the last acts in a long history of service to the Scottish nation by a talented and distinguished family.

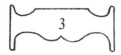

"THE GREAT SQUARE BUILDING":
the creation of Mylne's Court

As described in the first chapter, Robert Mylne's normal procedure when engaged in building operations was to buy up dilapidated and ruinous property, clear the ground on which it stood, and then rebuild. This practice he duly followed in the Lawnmarket. It is impossible to determine the exact details of the assortment of buildings which occupied the site before he started work, but an Inventory of Writs preserved among the Moses papers in the City of Edinburgh archives provides information on four of the pieces of property involved.

The first of these, a tenement which formed part of the street front, was purchased by Mylne from a James Muir: the earliest recorded owner of this property was a merchant, John Lourie, who sold it in 1612 to another merchant, Henry Seton; from him it passed to the Muir family in 1642. "A fore-part of a house and bigging* of a tenement of land"[8] was bought from James Henderson, a Writer to the Signet, and a further undefined tenement from William Stevenson, merchant, and Daniel Nicolson, writer: ownership of these two properties is known from 1638 and 1647 respectively. Mylne's fourth purchase, which is recorded in greater detail, appears to have been a very old tenement also forming part of the street front. It is first found in records in 1478, when part of it was in the possession of William Thomson, a merchant burgess of Edinburgh. In the late 1540s it was altered and perhaps even partially rebuilt, presumably after suffering damage in the 'Rough Wooing'. Thereafter, different owners gradually extended the property, buying up a quarter of a tenement here and half a backland there, so that by the middle of the seventeenth century it included not only a "tenement of land,

* *bigging*: outbuilding

19

back and fore, under and above", comprising "a Hall and Kitchine, Chamber Gallery, with a Loft and middle Chamber Gallery above the saids Chambers, and another Gallery and three laigh Cellers in the Ground ... entering by a Fore-gate off the Fore-Street", but also "a Fore high Booth and Back Booth ... also entering off the High Street", an "Under Dwelling House entering in the Closs called Cranstoun's Closs ... and another Dwelling House above the said Laigh House, entering also by the said Cranstoun's Closs". Such was the somewhat composite property acquired by the merchant John Moffat in 1641, and sold by his grandson Thomas to Robert Mylne some fifty years later.

As a result of these various purchases Mylne had acquired by 1690 sufficient adjacent property to allow a start to be made on the building of his new court. Almost immediately, however, he ran into trouble with his new neighbours, as a petition to the Privy Council from William Douglas of Mortoune and his wife Mary Bourshar relates. Mary was the owner of an adjoining tenement, which had been in her family's possession for forty years. On 21 July 1690, she recounts, Robert Mylne brought in workmen and

"did cutt off all the stoups* whereupon the forestair stood, and since hes digged beneath the ground fyve or six els deep seeking ane foundatione, and besyds hes not only tirled the back syde by takeing away the scleets, but lykewayes hes robbed and away taken all boards, dails, parple, nails, fixed work and doors, the which unchristiane useadge never haveing been advertised did give such ane surpryseall to the saids petitioners and their tennents, haveing gotten nottice of the forsaid stoups and undermynding of the saids ground, that they were forced all to flee and run away, albeit the saids petitioners nor there tennents did not know of neyther house nor hall to go to".[9]

Mylne was certainly not above unscrupulous behaviour at times: in 1678 the Town Council had complained that he was neglecting one of their commissions in favour of some private work and withheld payment from him, in 1701 he was fined 500 merks for "the unwarrantable hight of the new buildings on the south syde of

* *stoups*: wooden posts; *tirled*: upset; *scleets*: slates; *dails*: wooden planks; *parple*: partition walls

the parliament closs",[10] and in 1703 he was further disciplined for building too far into the street at the Luckenbooths* and having "in a most Clandastine maner incroached upon the touns propertie".[11] Building regulations have always created annoying restrictions for those with great ideas, and Mary Bourshar may well have been in the right. The Privy Council, however, refused to grant her petition to have all work stopped until the case could be heard, and ordained Mylne to continue with his project.

Further legal problems lay ahead. It would appear that the purchase of the composite property from Thomas Moffat took some time to complete, and that Mylne had been somewhat precipitate in demolishing it. At all events, in June 1692 Moffat complained that Mylne had "by qt order I know not razed from top to bottom ane tenement of land and merchant's shop pertaneing and belonging to me".[12] As he claimed damages from Mylne for "the razeing and downpulling of my said tenement" but was shortly to leave Scotland on business, Moffat appointed to look after his interests the wealthy and influential merchant George Watson, the same George Watson whose later gifts to his city were to place him amongst her greatest benefactors. The dispute appears to have been amicably settled, and in 1698 the transfer of Moffat's "Tenement of Land . . . all lately demolished and cast down . . . and the Grounds respective thereof, now comprehended within [the] great Square Building"[13] was finally completed, George Watson signing the disposition on Moffat's behalf.

In all of this building work, Mylne's partner was Andrew Paterson of Kirkton, one of the burgh's leading wrights. The precise nature of their partnership is uncertain, but the importance of Paterson's role is suggested by many of the relevant contemporary documents, which give the same prominence to his name as to Mylne's. Other important facts relating to the building of Mylne's Court are likewise unknown: the cost of the project, the size and nature of the labour force, the time taken to complete the building. Unknown too, surprisingly, is the actual extent of the work which Mylne carried out. While he is rightly given the credit for developing the idea of having a square of tenements opening on

* *Luckenbooths*: a rambling block of tenements and shops situated between the north wall of St Giles and the High Street

to a central courtyard, it must not automatically be assumed that he actually built all four sides of the square.

He was certainly responsible for building the south block with its frontage on the Lawnmarket and for clearing the open space behind; he very probably carried out some internal refurbishing in the north and east blocks; but that may have been all. The now demolished west side of the square was indubitably older than 1690, and the east side is dated to the early seventeenth century by the members of the Royal Commission on the Ancient Monuments of Scotland in their inventory of monuments in the City of Edinburgh. Over the north side there is disagreement: the Commissioners describe it as contemporary with Mylne's south block, whereas a number of other authorities state that it is a century earlier, the *Third Statistical Account* going so far as to assign to it the exact date of 1590. It is quite conceivable that in the warren of buildings occupying this part of the town Mylne found that these three old structures, already forming by accident three sides of a square, fitted in with his plans: all he then had to do was to clear the space between these three buildings and the Lawnmarket and complete the square by putting up what is now its south side.*

Whatever the actual details of the building, the square had come into being as a result of Mylne's vision, and it was perfectly proper to attach his name to it. 'Mylne's Court' has been its normal designation from its earliest days: other names appearing in older documents and maps are 'Mill's Square', 'Mylne's Square at the Bowhead' (to distinguish it from the other Mylne's Square: the head, or upper end, of the West Bow joined the Lawnmarket directly opposite Mylne's Court), and once, 'Lindsay's Square foregainst the weigh-house', presumably after one of its first inhabitants, David Lindsay. Entry from the street was obtained through two pends, one at each end of the new south wing. The passage which still exists today was called Cranston's Close, the name being taken from an adjacent tenement belonging to James Cranston: this provided a through route from the Lawnmarket to the old road running beside the Nor' Loch. The other entry, which like Cranston's Close sloped steeply downwards from south to north, was a cul-de-sac known as Mylne's Entry, Mylne's Close, or

* A ground plan of Mylne's Court in 1690 is given in fig. 2(i).

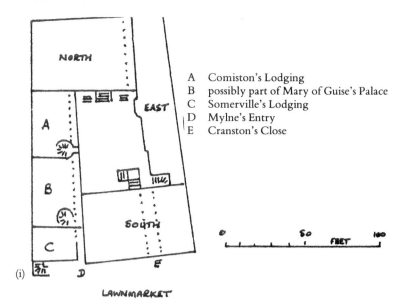

A Comiston's Lodging
B possibly part of Mary of Guise's Palace
C Somerville's Lodging
D Mylne's Entry
E Cranston's Close

(i)   Mylne's Court in 1690
(ii) Mylne's Court after demolition of the west side in 1883, showing house numbers
(iii) Mylne's Court after restoration in 1970

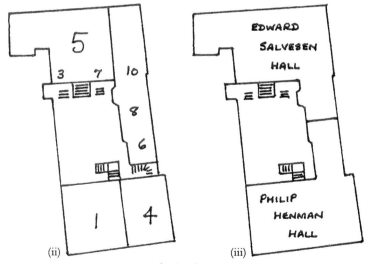

Mylne's Court
Three stages of development

Bell's Close: it disappeared when the west side of the square was demolished in 1883.

The stranger who made his way through one of these passages into Mylne's new courtyard must have been immediately struck by the contrast between the imposing buildings on its north, east, and south sides and the very different appearance of the houses on the west, whose demolition undoubtedly robbed Mylne's Court of some of its character. Of the two houses on this side which looked into the courtyard, the northern one was the town mansion of the Lairds of Comiston. A five-storey building dating at least from the early seventeenth century, its timber gables were a conspicuous feature, as was the little wooden bridge over Mylne's Entry which gave access from the courtyard to the main doorway. Over this door was a lintel carved with the inscription 'Blessit be God in al his Giftis: 1580'; this stone is now incorporated in the passageway of the Assembly Hall built on the same site. The neighbouring house was a very old land; during the demolition, through-going doors were discovered in its west walls, indicating that it was part of a much larger building, very possibly the 'Palace' of Mary of Guise, mother of Mary Queen of Scots: this mansion was most probably built immediately after the burning of Edinburgh in 1544, and served as Mary's residence during the period of her regency in the 1550s.

At the south-west corner of Mylne's Court, completing its west side but not actually forming part of the courtyard, was perhaps the most striking house of the three: Somerville's Land. It was an attractive three-storey building, with a timber frontage which extended out over the pavement, each storey projecting a little further than the one below; the roof had a row of three timber gables of different heights. Such extensive use of timber was, of course, a feature of the early days of the Old Town, and may still be seen at John Knox's House in the High Street. Like John Knox's House, too, Somerville's Land had a fore-stair from the street giving access to the first floor of the building. It is likely that its upper floors were built not long after 1544, but the stone-vaulted basement was much older: during the demolition, traces were found of the original level of the Lawnmarket about eight feet below that of the present pavement. One of the rooms on the second floor had a painted ceiling. In view of the later connection between this area and both the University of Edinburgh and the Church, it is worth noting that a member of the family whose property this was, Bartholomew Somerville, was one of the University's earliest benefactors. In 1639 the University received from him, according to its historian Craufurd, "the greatest accession of its patrimony which ever had been bestowed by any private person",[14] namely, in the words of Somerville's deed, "the soume of tuentie sex thousand merks, tuentie thousand merks ... for intertaynement of ane professor of divinitie in King James his Colledge ... and the soume of sex thousand merks to be imployed for building of ane house to the said professor",[15] the house for whose construction Robert Mylne's uncle, John, was responsible.

The other three sides of the new courtyard were more uniform. On the east side, what is now to be seen is almost entirely a twentieth-century reconstruction, part of the original structure having been demolished after a fire in 1912 and the remainder taken down during the major renovation of the 1960s: only the base of the projecting octagonal tower with its turnpike stair is original, the bold moulding of its doorway being the principal evidence for the early seventeenth-century date for this side of the court. Nonetheless, this reconstruction recaptures faithfully the general spirit, if not the exact detail, of the original: old drawings show this side as consisting of two parts, as at present, but with the division between them occurring several feet further south and with the southern portion rising one storey higher than the northern. The principal modern addition is the dormer windows: previously there was only one of these, on the higher portion of the roof at the south end of the block.

Whether the north block was actually built by Mylne or not, it is clear from the fact that he was able to sell the flats inside as desirable new residences that he was responsible at least for thoroughly refurbishing it. Like its neighbour on the east, it rose five storeys above the courtyard, and originally had fewer dormer windows on its southern side. There is a handsome central doorway, whose mouldings are in the form of a very flat ogee arch, a type of ornamentation found elsewhere among Mylne's work. On each side of the steps up to this doorway is a shorter flight leading down to a small basement area giving access to the flats below courtyard level. The northern elevation of this side of the court is dramatic, with an interesting skyline of massive chimney stalks and dormer windows set in picturesquely crow-stepped gables. The ground here falls away very steeply, allowing room for two further floors below the basement level of the courtyard: this nine-storey building must have been a starkly impressive sight at the top of the steep slope up from the Nor' Loch.

The fourth side of the square is Mylne's new ashlar-fronted tenement of 1690, six storeys high to both front and rear, with original dormer windows in both roofs, one of those at the back being set in an intriguingly asymmetrical crow-stepped gable. This building was originally in two distinct parts, separated internally by a thick dividing wall, each half having its own entrance and staircase. The western part was reached, as today, by a short outside stair from the courtyard, while the entrance to the eastern part was from Cranston's Close, where an outside stair led up to first floor level; thereafter, the two common stairs ran in parallel to the upper storeys of the building. Both of the outside stairs had 'bell-cast' balustrades, i.e. they are moulded in an outward-curving loop to make the stair more easily negotiable — so the story goes — by crinoline-gowned ladies.

Such were the buildings surrounding the spacious quadrangle which provided their inhabitants with much-needed breathing-space, light, and fresh air. Almost all of the property consisted of private accommodation, with two exceptions. Two rooms and a cellar in the basement of the north block, entering from Cranston's Close (what is now the Warden's study and the lower part of the adjoining common room) is described in the title deeds as a 'Warehouse' and at one time was the premises of David Todd, a house painter. More significantly, the ground floor of the south block was occupied by a line of shops. This highly desirable juxtaposition of commercial and residential property was typical of many an early Scottish townscape, though sadly over the years the value of such an arrangement has not always been fully realised. Establishments of several different kinds have operated from this building, the present public-house having a particularly long and distinguished ancestry.

The upper floors of the south block contained ten flats, the five western ones reached by the main entrance in the courtyard and the other five from the stair in Cranston's Close. Most flats were of six or seven 'fire rooms' (i.e. rooms with a fireplace): a description of one of the flats on the west lists two bedchambers and a dining room overlooking the Lawnmarket, and a 'dark room', a kitchen, and a third bedchamber looking into the courtyard. The north block contained twelve flats, one entered from each of the basement areas mentioned above, and one on each side of the common stair on the five upper storeys (now known as levels 4 to 8). Most of these flats had seven fire rooms; one of the ground floor flats had only six, the main entrance to the building occupying the space of the seventh room, and the top floor flats were rather smaller, having only four fire rooms.

The attics and cellars were subdivided and portions allotted to each of the flats in the building. Associated with one flat, for example, was "a cellar consisting of seven feet broad and fourteen feet long lying in the ground of the ... back building ... and having stone partitions round the same, together with a garret above the scale stairs with a chimney and stone windows therein, which garret consists of six foot broad betwixt the gavils,* and twelve foot long".[16] In later years, some of the larger cellars became properties in their own right. Associated with the basement flat on the west of the north block, for example, were two cellars, one twenty-four feet square on the same level as the flat and another of the same size immediately below, approached from Mylne's Entry: the upper one was converted into two apartments and a closet, and together with the cellar below certainly formed a separate entity by 1870, when Patrick Considine, formerly a provision dealer in the Lawnmarket, sold it to William Dickson, a wholesale merchant from Argyle Square. Not all cellars and garrets were thus separated from their flats, however: a photograph of the Lawnmarket entrance to Mylne's Court taken in the early years of this century shows a notice advertising for sale "No. 1 Milne Court, eastmost half of first flat with one attic room and cellars in Court".

Internally, all of the buildings have been altered to such an extent that it is not possible to recover the exact layout of the flats on each floor. Nevertheless, in the north block at least, sufficient original features survive — or have been carefully restored — to

* *gavils*: end-walls

27

provide a tantalising glimpse of late seventeenth-century life. On entering the main doorway, one is confronted by a broad scale-and-platt* stair leading to the upper floors: this type of staircase is much more spacious and convenient than the winding turnpike which was then the normal kind of stair in ordinary domestic premises, and Mylne's use of this feature in his new buildings was one of their greatest attractions.

On each landing are what were originally the outer doors of two flats: these were of thick oak, studded with nails, and often decorated with painting: the door on the east side of the landing beside the main entrance (now level 4) is original and has traces of painting, while other original doors are on level 5 above. On each landing was a foot-scraper, very necessary after fighting one's way through the filth of the streets, and even of the courtyard and the stairs, for regular stair-cleaning was still unknown; the modern replicas serve as floor-numbers.

Despite considerable internal reorganisation in the 1960s, a number of rooms remain intact. In the flat on the west side of level 5, erroneously believed to have been reserved by Mylne for his own use (he in fact sold it to a merchant by the name of Balfour), one room has been restored to its presumed seventeenth-century state. Its wooden door still has the customary latch, now curiously baffling to twentieth-century minds, and the room within is of a surprisingly small size, when it is considered that this was the drawing-room of a desirable town residence. The walls are very thick, and panelled, with delicate wooden carving around a stone fireplace. The rich frieze and the ornate moulding in the domed ceiling of a wall-niche, both of wood in an intricate floral design, have not survived the passage of the years and the predatory attentions of twentieth-century vandals, but a large enough fragment of the frieze remains to show that the modern plaster representation is extremely faithful to the original. The new wooden floorboards are cut in a variety of lengths and widths, mindful of the days before mechanical tools brought the dreariness of uniformity to such things, while the heads of the nails show through the face of the wood, another original feature carefully followed in the recent restoration. Close to this room, along

---

* *scale-and-platt*: stairs and landing

corridors with uneven rough-cast walls, is the kitchen of Balfour's flat. It has a baking oven with grooves on the side walls to carry the trays and a massive fireplace with holes in the sides to hold the spit and holes on the upper rim for the hooks on which Mrs Balfour would hang her kettles and pans. Other large fireplaces of similar kind still exist in several parts of the building.

A number of rooms have panelled walls, and this feature was presumably fairly widespread in the original building. Less common, surely, was a feature which still survives in a flat on the east side of level 4: a room with its panelled walls painted to resemble marble. Some panels are covered with swirls of a dull, muted green, others display bold tiger-skin browns and oranges. This style of decoration was brought back from Italy by Inigo Jones, and was not uncommon in England: it did not, however, commend itself to the more muted taste of the Scots, and this example — retouched of course in the 1960s — is one of the very few still in existence. Another was discovered recently during the demolition of Stockwell Mansion, Glasgow, which was built around 1686.

One external feature which immediately attracts attention is the number of tiny shuttered windows. These are known as 'powder-closet' or 'prayer-cell' windows, the tiny room behind being used originally as a place of retreat in which the head of the household was wont to perform his private devotions: so important was the religious lead expected from the father of a family that such 'prayer-cells' became standard features in house-building of the late seventeenth and early eighteenth centuries. Later, when more attention was paid to body than to soul, the alternative use of these rooms as powder-closets no doubt became more prevalent. The upper half of each window is glazed, and the lower half is open; as both halves are shuttered, various permutations permitting light and fresh air are possible. During the reconstruction of the 1960s one of the original windows was discovered: the glass in it had been set directly into the stonework, which must have allowed moisture to seep through, creating a measure of discomfort for the in-habitants.

It was customary for the old Edinburgh tenements to provide homes for a wide variety of social classes, the gentry normally occupying the central floors with their poorer neighbours above and below them. One illustration of this is provided by the size of the windows in the north block: those on levels 5 and 6 are taller than those on levels 3, 4 and 7, providing brighter rooms for a better class of resident. Another instance of the way class-consciousness affected building practice is seen in the central stairway, where the vertical rises are decoratively moulded from levels 4 to 7 but are plain elsewhere.

None of the original advertisements for the property survives, but it is highly likely that Mylne was as proud of his Court as he was of his Square: it too would surely add both "to the decorment of the good Town" and "to the great convenience and accommodation of his Majesty's lieges".

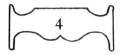

"A FACETIOUS SET OF CITIZENS":
the original residents

One of the most exciting features of life in the tenements of the Old Town was the social mix which prevailed among the residents. All classes of people, churchmen and lawyers, nobility and tradesmen, lived together in the one building and rubbed shoulders on the common stair. Mylne's Court was no exception, and those who made their homes there in the early 1690s represented a wide variety of trades and callings.

In each part of the new south block, there were five storeys above the shops; there ought, therefore, to have been space for ten families. No records remain, however, of any residents in either of the top floors, and it seems likely that these were used to provide particularly commodious attic space for the flats below. The first inhabitants of the remaining eight flats are all known.

On the stairway which entered from Cranston's Close, the first floor flat was bought by Robert Cairns, a wright, for 3222 merks,* for which sum he acquired not only a flat of four fire rooms but also the use of two underground cellars. Cairns and his wife had four children, Andrew, Robert, Elizabeth, and Christian, "two whereof are at home in the Hous and the other two nursing at Swanston and Cameron",[17] it being reasonably common for children to be boarded out with a wet-nurse. Also in the flat there lived two servant women, an apprentice who was a permanent lodger, and "three journeymen who are not constant servants but somtymes serving others".

Above them lived the Bairds: Alexander Baird was a merchant, and his more spacious accommodation of seven fire rooms and two

---

* A merk was two-thirds of a pound Scots, which was one-half of a pound sterling. In the following pages, sums are quoted variously in merks or in pounds Scots, reflecting a similar variation in the sources.

closets had cost him 5500 merks. Five children, two servants, and an apprentice made up the household, with another child, Patrick, "nursing at the Pleughlands in the West Church Paroch".

The next flat on this stair was bought by James McLurgg, later Sir James McLurgg of Vogrie, who had previously lived further down the Lawnmarket in Gladstone's Land, and moved to a bigger flat in the more prestigious Mylne's Court on its completion. With him came his wife Marion, her grandniece "whom she has keeped thir seven year and more", a man servant ("at £12 a year and two pairs of shoes") and two women servants. The family was well-known in Edinburgh, two of McLurgg's nieces being proprietors of one of the most popular coffee-houses of the time.

Finally, the flat on the fourth floor was owned by an advocate, John Stewart of Ascog, whose wife Margaret was a daughter of John Robertson, apothecary to Charles II; they had five children and two servants.

The other half of the south block, entered from the courtyard, was occupied entirely by merchants. On the first floor were David Lindsay and his son Alexander, both traders of some substance, together with Mrs Lindsay senior, two men servants, and three women servants, one of whom was in Alexander's employ. Next came Laurence Gellatly with his wife, two young daughters, and maidservant; they also had a lodger, one William Archibald, a writer. Above them lived Michael Allan, his wife, an apprentice, and two servants, and on the fourth floor John Hunter, with his wife and three servants.

Records are less complete for the refurbished block on the east side of the court. The two flats on the first floor were sold to Thomas Kilgour, a mason, and his wife, and to Walter Melville, an employee of the Lyon Court who held the offices of Rothesay Herald from 1697 to 1718 and Herald Painter from 1700 to 1724. His wife, four children all under the age of six (another had recently died), two apprentices, presumably apprentice painters, and two servants shared a flat which had only four fire rooms. One of the flats on the second floor was bought by James Miln, an apothecary who was apparently no relation to the builder, but no further information is available on the other early residents in this block.

The first occupants of all twelve flats in the north block are known. On the west side the basement flat was bought by James Hunter, a baker, who lived there with his wife, four children under sixteen (two older children lived away from home in Liberton), an apprentice, two men servants, and two women servants: the seven small rooms must have been rather crowded at times. The other basement flat was the property of John Mouat of Balquhally, an advocate.

The upper flats were all reached by the common stair. Immediately above the Hunters lived David Callander, a lawyer, with his wife, six children, and two women servants. Next came James Balfour, a prosperous merchant listed in the 1694 Poll Tax Returns as "worth 10,000 merks". An ancestor of Robert Louis Stevenson, his household consisted of his wife, five children, an apprentice, and two female servants. The flat above Balfour was bought by Dr William Blackadder, who held the office of 'King's Physician to the Forces' from 1690 to 1693, and above him lived Rev. James Webster and his first wife, Margaret Keir, along with her niece Margaret Watson and two servants: Elizabeth Webster was paid "£14 a year and two pairs of shoes", but the other servant, Margaret Whitehead, being under sixteen, was unpaid. The top flat was the property of James Byres, one of the town's leading merchants.

On the east side of the common stair, the flats were occupied by, again in ascending order, Lilias Gemmell, widow of Alexander Anderson, a coppersmith; Robert Munro, an advocate; Alexander Gibson of Durie, one of the Principal Clerks of Session; Hugh Cunningham, a Writer to the Signet; and Patrick Coutts, a merchant. These flats, too, had a full total of occupants: the Gibson household included a wife and three children, a nurse for one of the children (costing £25 per quarter), a manservant, and three women servants, while below him lived Munro, his wife, one of his two children (the other boarded at Duddingston), his mother-in-law, his sister-in-law, and two female servants: small wonder that the wry note is added to his tax return "and lest he should be like the wise men of Gotham he also counts himself paying pole as an advocat". Munro's wife, Anna Gledstanes, was a granddaughter of Thomas Gledstanes, the prosperous merchant who in 1617 bought and renovated the property further down the Lawnmarket still known as Gladstone's Land.

Several of these first residents were notable figures in the Edinburgh of the late seventeenth century and were elected by their fellows to a variety of important positions of responsibility. James McLurgg was one of the three candidates for Lord Provost in 1691 (on being unsuccessful, he made a series of bitter protests to the Privy Council concerning the conduct of the election), while at the other end of the social scale the guild of bakers elected James Hunter to be their Deacon for 1689-91. Baird, Allan, and Balfour were Merchant Councillors, and these three also served as Bailies, as did McLurgg and Lindsay: 'Baron Bailie of the West Port and Potterrow' was a high-sounding office held by Lindsay in 1684, and several of the others were also elected Baron Bailies of different parts of the burgh. McLurgg and Allan both held one of the highest positions of responsibility, that of Dean of Guild, McLurgg for 1689-91 and again for 1699-1701, and Allan for 1691-3: in this capacity they also represented Edinburgh as one of her two Commissioners to the General Convention of Burghs. Among McLurgg's other distinctions were his appointments as Master of the Merchant Company in 1695, and as a Commissioner of Supply for Edinburgh in 1702 and 1704.

Contemporary records leave no doubt as to the respectability of many of these citizens. Michael Allan was elected Kirk Treasurer for the year 1687, and in 1691 James Balfour was appointed to the same office. In this important capacity Balfour was much exercised over the state of Edinburgh's poor, and succeeded in raising additional funds for their benefit by imposing extra charges on funerals "held other than the ordinary time of 2 p.m."[18] The funeral of at least one of the original residents did not incur this penalty: in October 1696 Adam Blackadder "earnestly entreated" William Aikman of Carnie "to accompany the body of Mr William Blackadder, Doctor of Medicine, my brother, from his lodging in Miln's Squair at the head of the West Bow to his burial place in the Grayfriars upon Towsday the 27th instant at two afternoon".[19]

John Mouat and James McLurgg showed themselves to be particularly exemplary citizens by coming to the rescue of the Town Council when it was being hard-pressed by impatient creditors: in 1692 Mouat lent 4000 merks and in 1694 McLurgg lent £8000 to pay off pressing debts, the first of several such sums he was to make available over the next twenty years. At his death, McLurgg left much of his property to various "pious uses": "three thousand merks ... for mentaining of a bursar or student of Theologie at the Colledge of Edinburgh;"[20] "... to the common poor of Edinburgh, 4000 merks; ... to help ane that keeps a school for learning young boys to read and write whose parents are not able to help them, 3000 merks".[21] David Lindsay was another who expressed his generosity in a similar way, mortifying the sum of 500 merks to Trinity Hospital for the use of the poor. What the rich widow Anderson did with her money is not recorded, but she appears to have been a person of considerable substance. In addition to her flat in Mylne's Court, she owned parts of Stevenson's Land and Carrubber's Close, both further down the Royal Mile, and at the time of the 1696/7 Annuity Tax her assessment was approximately four times as high as that of any of her neighbours.

The proportion of merchants among this representative group of Old Town residents is a clear indication of the importance of trade in the Scottish economy of the time. A number of them had close links with commercial partners across the North Sea: Baird, for example, was a shareholder in a joint stock company trading between Scotland, Sweden, and Holland, of which his father-in-law had been one of the three founders. McLurgg was another who had close connections with the continent, and kept up a voluminous correspondence with Andrew Russell, the Scottish factor in Rotterdam (his nieces' coffee-house, he writes on one occasion, "stands in neid of some Coffie berrie. I desire you to cause try the lowest pryce and buy ane barrell full of it that will hold 100 or 150 lb."[22]). McLurgg had begun his career as a general merchant, with a small side-line in discounting bills of exchange, but by 1690 the bill-broking side of his business had expanded so considerably that he was able to live off its profits and give up ordinary trading altogether.

James Balfour was particularly active in trying to promote Scottish trade overseas. After the Scots Parliament passed the Act for Encouraging Foreign Trade in 1693, he spent a great deal of time and energy — and money — trying to arouse enthusiasm for the establishment of a trading company. When this dream came to fruition (not entirely through Balfour's efforts) and "The

Company of Scotland Trading to Africa and the Indies" was established in 1695, Balfour duly claimed some of the credit and submitted to the first meeting of the directors his bill for £2119 12s 8d in respect of services already rendered. He might have been less sanguine about the new Company had he known that it would result in that disastrous enterprise known as the Darien Scheme, which was to bring Scotland close to the brink of economic ruin. The establishment of the Company and the prospect of the foundation of an overseas colony created an unprecedented amount of interest, and when a Subscription Book was opened in February 1696 in the Company's offices in Mylne's Square Balfour was among the crowds who queued up on the first day to offer their support. Several of his neighbours shared his enthusiasm: James Byres' name also appears among the first subscribers, while McLurgg and Cunningham subscribed on the second day, to be followed by Michael Allan, Alexander Gibson, and even James Miln the apothecary. Robert Mylne was another supporter of the venture.

In all the sorry events that ensued one of the most inglorious parts was to be played by James Byres. His early support for the Company had apparently been motivated by the hope that his name would be remembered when the time came for official appointments in the colony to be made. When the first expedition sailed for South America in July 1698, Byres was not of its number, but in the summer of 1699 he was chosen as one of the four Councillors, "men of special trust", who were to direct the second expedition. This body of supposed reinforcements arrived in Darien in November, only to find that the colony had been abandoned several months before. Byres' fellow-Councillors proved to be too spineless to cope with this unexpected situation, and his became the ruling voice in the Council: had he been a different sort of person, the history of the colony might have been different, but a "cowardly, dishonourable, self-opinionated puppy",[23] as a contemporary described him, does not usually provide the right calibre of leadership in a crisis. For two months the disheartened settlers struggled on, Byres' contentious personality proving no help to them in their fight against disease, hunger, and apathy. Finally, self-interest proved victorious, and at the first hint of hostilities from the Spanish Byres deserted the colony,

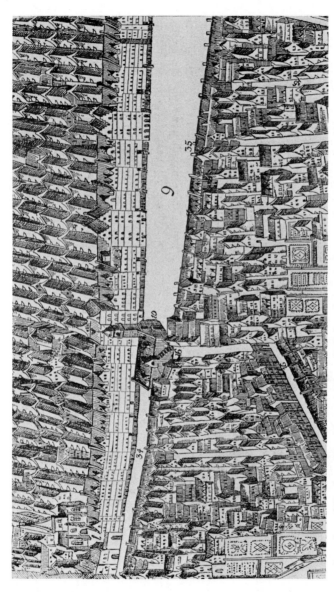

1 A section of Gordon of Rothiemay's Plan of Edinburgh (1647), showing the High Street (9) narrowing into the Lawnmarket (34). The building in the centre of the street at the head of the West Bow (16) is the Weigh House (10), and the site of the future Mylne's Court is immediately behind it (see p. 3).

2 The west side of Mylne's Court in the early nineteenth century, from a painting by Henry Duguid, showing the Comiston mansion and the neighbouring house (see p. 24).

3 The Lawnmarket frontage of Mylne's Court, 1883: Somerville's Land (see pp. 24–5) is to the left.

4 Mylne's Court in the early 1900s, from a photograph by F. M. Chrystal.

conveniently forgetting his virtual position as its Governor, and took ship for Jamaica: two months later, Darien was abandoned for the second time, and Scotland's hopes of prosperity from her overseas colony were shattered. Byres' ignominious contribution to the failure of the enterprise earned him a condemnation from the Company's Directors, who found him guilty of "several unwarrantable, arbitrary, illegal, and inhumane practices, manifestly tending to the great and irretrievable loss of the Company and the Colony, and to the dishonour of the nation".[24] This rebuke had no effect on the man: his mercantile activities continued as before, and he died at sea in 1706 while returning from a trading venture to Portugal.

Important though all these merchants were in the life of both city and nation, they were not the only noteworthy figures among the early residents in the Court. The professional classes were represented by a clutch of lawyers and by Rev. James Webster. Alexander Gibson of Durie came of a particularly notable legal family, and was in fact descended from the brother of William Gibson, Dean of Restalrig, who had been one of the original Senators of the College of Justice along with Abbot Alexander Mylne in 1532. Alexander Gibson's grandfather, Lord Durie, had also been a Senator and was Lord President of the Court in 1642-3; by his marriage to Margaret, daughter of Sir Thomas Craig, author of *Jus Feudale*, Durie became connected with one of the most eminent legal writers of the seventeenth century. His son, Sir Alexander Gibson, father of the Alexander who lived in Mylne's Court, became a Clerk of Council and Session in 1632 and Lord Clerk Register in 1641, being knighted by Charles I earlier in the same year; in 1646 he was raised to the bench, but was deprived of his offices in the political storms of 1649. The Alexander of Mylne's Court followed in the family tradition, and in 1688 published *Durie's Practicks*, a compendium of his grandfather's decisions over twenty years of judicial work. His son Thomas (who married a daughter of the renowned Colonel Tam Dalyell of the Scots Guards) was Principal Clerk of Session from 1726 until his death in 1779.

Perhaps the most colourful of all these first inhabitants of the Court was the Rev. James Webster, minister of the second charge in the Tolbooth parish from 1693 until his death in 1720. In early

37

life he had been imprisoned for his faith on three occasions, and during his twenty-seven years' ministry at the Tolbooth he acquired a reputation for outspokenness. In 1712 he had a judicial process instituted against him by the celebrated wit, poet, and physician, Dr Archibald Pitcairne, whom he had called an atheist, and in 1717, during the prosecution on charges of Arminianism of John Simson, who despite being Professor of Divinity in the University of Glasgow "loved to hover on the brink of heresy",[25] Webster "worked himself into such an extremity of passion that there was a probability of his being deposed by the Assembly at their next sitting, had he not tendered an apology".[26] By his third wife, Agnes Menzies, he had three children, the eldest of whom, Alexander, was to become one of Mylne's Court's most distinguished sons. Born in 1707, he was minister of the Tolbooth parish from 1737 until 1784, preaching to such packed congregations that it was said that "it was easier to get a seat in the Kingdom of Heaven than in the Tolbooth Kirk".[27] He was in the forefront of the movement to secure better financial provision for ministers' widows and children; he produced the first 'census' or enumeration of the people of Scotland in 1755; he was instrumental in pressing both for the building of the New Town and for the opening up of the Highlands; and he was laden with ecclesiastical honours — Chaplain to the Prince of Wales in 1748, Moderator of the General Assembly in 1753, Doctor of Divinity in 1760, and finally Chaplain to George III and Dean of the Chapel Royal. Anecdotes about him abound, many based on the fact that "he combined what would now seem the incongruous elements of a highly popular evangelical divine with the manners and accomplishments of a man of the world. . . . In an age when hard drinking was habitual with all classes, his powers of endurance enabled him to enjoy society with impunity".[28] The story is told of a friend overtaking him early one morning as he made his way home after an obviously convivial evening. "Ay, doctor, what wad the auld wives o' the Tolbooth say if they saw you noo?" asked his friend, to which the good doctor retorted, "Tuts, man, they wadna believe their e'en." Boswell and Johnson met him both before and after their tour to the Hebrides: "Webster", says Boswell, "though not learned, had such a knowledge of mankind, such a fund of information and entertainment, so clear a head and such accommodating manners, that Dr. Johnson found him a very agreeable companion":[29] rare praise indeed.

Some indication of the life-style of these early inhabitants can be pieced together from the inventories of their possessions drawn up after their deaths for executory purposes. The public rooms were simply furnished with a practical assortment of tables and chairs and other items of everyday furniture. The walls were hung with coloured curtains; Hugh Cunningham had "blew hingings"[30] in his smaller front room while his neighbour John Stewart had a variety of green and embroidered hangings including some made from gilded leather. Cunningham also possessed some finer items, such as his dining room clock which was valued at the considerable sum of £108, and a selection of silver and pewter table-ware: "2 small silver boxes for pepper and mustard, a silver salt 2 oz 5½ drops, one pair of snuffers, a dozen pewter trenchers". Mirrors adorned some of the rooms, and it was thought worth remarking that one of Stewart's cabinets was made of olive wood, although this, like the gilded leather hangings, remained unsold after the rest of his possessions were disposed of by roup.

Particular attention is paid in these testamentary inventories to linen, which was obviously highly prized and valued: indeed, Sir James McLurgg included in his will "a memorandum . . . as to the division of his linen and silver", part of what he owned being left to his neighbour James Miln. In a number of inventories, linen of all kinds is carefully listed, in surprisingly large quantities. Included in one household's collection, for example, were eight dozen napkins and a wide variety of bed sheets and blankets, table cloths and towels. The beds themselves were usually hung with curtains and both the mattresses and pillows were feather-filled. The kitchen utensils were generally of copper or pewter: the tea kettle, the frying pan, the salt bucket, the goosing iron,* and even "ane little pott". Chimney pieces were detachable and had grates suitable for cooking on: Stewart had "two old chimneys in the fore room and the other in the litle mide roome with a banock iron".

Such were the worldly goods with which those first inhabitants of Mylne's new court were endowed: those humble tradesmen,

---

* *goosing iron*: a smoothing iron; *bannock iron*: a type of griddle which was suspended over a fire and on which bannocks (a kind of oatcake) were baked

sharp legal minds, kenspeckle city worthies, and merchant adventurers who exchanged pleasantries with each other on the common stair and whose children revelled in the variety of new games which the freedom of a courtyard permitted. A busy and bustling place it must have been, with a bright future.

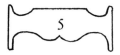

"AS EXTRAORDINARY AS THE SCENE":
the eighteenth and nineteenth centuries

The previous chapter emphasised the diversity that characterised the first inhabitants of Mylne's Court. It might also have laid stress on their sense of community, one of the more significant features of life in the Old Town tenements and courts: with several houses opening on to the same stair, and a number of common stairs meeting in the one courtyard, it was impossible not to talk to one's neighbour, to know some of his business, or to share in his leisure. Community life in the Lawnmarket was so strong that some of its occupants formed themselves into the 'Lawnmarket Club', and prided themselves on their reputation for being the first to hear any important item of news. They are described as being "a dram-drinking, news-mongering, facetious set of citizens, who met every morn about seven o'clock, and after proceeding to the post office to ascertain the news when the mail arrived, generally adjourned to a public-house and refreshed themselves with a libation of brandy".[31] Reputations, of course, had to be preserved at all costs, and not a few items of 'news' were concocted over the libations of brandy, to the extent that the term 'Lawnmarket Gazette' became a byword for "unfounded articles of intelligence spread abroad by roguish or waggish originators".

Within Mylne's Court, however, the residents were not entirely one big happy family. *The Decisions of the Lords of Council and Session*, under the date 7 January 1710, record how Michael Allan fell foul of his neighbours. His cellar was situated directly under Cranston's Close and its roof had suffered damage "by the loads and heavy carriages brought over it for the use of the back-tenements".[32] He applied to the Dean of Guild of the time, who inspected the damage, declared that the roof of the cellar was indeed "damnified", and instructed the owners of the adjacent property "to bear a proportional part of the expense in repairing it, extending to £100 Scots or thereby". They, however, under the leadership of Rev. James Webster, not surprisingly disputed this, on the grounds "that they had bought their houses from Mr Miln the builder with a clause in their dispositions of free ish* and entry, and so can no more be liable for repairing his cellar than any other of the lieges whose business leads them to resort to that court"; the pend was in any case a public thoroughfare through which anyone could pass. The Lords of the Session upheld Mr Webster's objection, sensibly pointing out that the Dean of Guild had been wrong in the first place in allowing Allan "to cover his cellar only with joists and pavement stone"; in a few years the wood would rot, and "a stone pend" should have been used.

It is not recorded whether Allan acted on this advice, but the underground vaults survive to the present day and have seen a variety of uses. The steep dip immediately to the north of the Lawnmarket gives them considerable depth — the equivalent of four storeys below street level in places. Arched bins for storing wine have been found in these vaults, pointing to their early use as wine cellars, partly for the benefit of the residents above, but partly also, no doubt, for the storing of contraband liquor smuggled into the city from the ports of Leith and Granton. The dark and mysterious subterranean passages gave rise to ghostly tales of tunnels linking the Castle with Holyrood and the Lawnmarket with Princes Street: one ex-resident of the twentieth century, recalling the escapades of his childhood, relates that "we all went so far down the tunnel one night, but we were so scared that we all ran out again: there were so many tunnels leading off one another that you could have a tour around Edinburgh".[33] Down the main tunnel a piper used to walk every night, playing vigorously to scare away anyone who might be planning to ambush the Castle. One night he never returned: some say he was eaten by rats, others claim that they can still hear him. During the Second World War the cellars and vaults were converted into air-raid shelters, and now, after the reconstruction of the 1960s, the boilerhouse for the Mylne's Court complex, including two tanks holding approximately 13,000 gallons of oil, occupies the space beneath the courtyard.

* *ish*: exit

In 1759, the harmonious life of the Court was again disrupted by another piece of unneighbourly wrangling. The west gable of the north block had been gradually sinking, and this had affected the floor levels in that part of the building, giving them a slight slope. The wall had finally to be taken down and completely rebuilt, and although the various owners all agreed to postpone the levelling of their floors until the new wall was completed one perverse character, William Walker, carried out his alterations in advance of this and then refused to take part in the subsequent general floor-raising exercise. Much time and energy were spent by the Dean of Guild Court in hearing petitions, preparing answers, visiting the site, and interviewing the various parties: Rev. Alexander Webster entered the fray and wrote "either the whole floors must be raised, or none of them can be raised, without destroying the form of the rooms altogether".[34] Reading the papers, one has the impression that a major issue of both social and structural significance is being fought over, until William Walker inadvertently lets slip that the amount by which the floors required to be raised was a mere two inches. The whole episode is then seen to be a typical example of the kind of trivial domestic upset to which tenement dwellers seem particularly attached.

Another, and happier, activity which has long been a favourite with tenement dwellers is watching the world go by. The residents in the south block of Mylne's Court were in a specially privileged position for observing the passing show, since for centuries the Lawnmarket and the High Street formed Edinburgh's principal thoroughfare, and the Lindsays, the McLurggs, the Allans, and their neighbours could look from their windows upon all the normal hustle and bustle of a capital city, enlivened from time to time by the ceremonial pomp and circumstance of special occasions. Movement of troops to and from the castle was a regular occurrence, and many a colourful procession of soldiers must have entranced the children, watching excitedly from up above. Much rarer, but no less of a public spectacle, were the occasions when witches were brought up the Lawnmarket from their place of confinement in the Tolbooth to be burnt at the upper end of Castlehill, a practice which continued until 1722.

Exactly one hundred years after the last witch had passed under their windows, the residents of Mylne's Court had a grandstand view of one of the city's most splendid ceremonial occasions. In August 1822, George IV paid a state visit to Edinburgh, the first of the Hanoverians to grace their northern capital with their royal presence. On Thursday 22 August Mylne's Court residents — and, no doubt, all their cousins from the country who had crowded into the city and were filling all available spare beds — would have been up early, for that afternoon the King was to ride in solemn procession from Holyrood House to the Castle. Not since Charles I's coronation at Holyrood in 1633 had Edinburgh been so gripped by royal fever, intensified on this occasion by the fact that the procession was to include the ancient regalia of Scotland, found only four years previously after having been mislaid within the Castle since the Union of the Parliaments in 1707. On that Thursday, although "the weather threatened all the morning to be very unfavourable",[35] every window in the Canongate, the High Street, and the Lawnmarket would have been thronged with citizens eager to see their monarch, who had so far been on view mainly at levées attended only by the gentry. The gentry on this occasion occupied special stands erected on the site of the Castle esplanade; their carriages brought them from the New Town to the top of the recently completed Mound, and deposited them immediately below the north block of Mylne's Court, whose residents were thus to some extent compensated for missing all the excitement in the Lawnmarket. Excitement was indeed the order of the day, as the capital's loyal citizens packed the streets. Outside Mylne's Court the Society of Chairmasters, whose members operated the city's sedan chairs, had been allocated space, and they made a colourful spectacle "with crosses on their breasts, heather or thistles in their hats, and most of them with rods in their hands".[36]

As the day drew on, the weather deteriorated, "the rain pouring in torrents, and only ceasing now and then for a moment or two to pour again with more violence":[35] the gentry under their fragile awnings might well have envied the humble folk at their windows in the Lawnmarket. The procession, however, went ahead as planned: trumpeters of the Mid-Lothian Yeomanry and a company of Breadalbanes and Macgregors, marching twelve abreast; the Lord Lyon and his Court, their tabards a blaze of colour in the rain; various detachments of 'Highland Gentlemen', equally colourful in the tartan that was so much a feature of the whole royal visit; the long-lost Sword of State, Sceptre, and Crown of Scotland; and finally, with only some further Highlanders — Drummonds and Sutherlands this time — and another squad of yeomanry behind him, the King himself. His Majesty was delighted with his welcome: "What a fine sight!" he is reported to have said on reaching the Castle, "and the people are as beautiful and as extraordinary as the scene". Never had the Lawnmarket seen the like, and great would be the talk that evening, as the day's events were told and retold round the kitchen ranges.

There was, however, much more for the residents of Mylne's Court to look out upon than merely the goings-on in the Royal Mile. Opposite the Court was the West Bow, a narrow, crooked street which opened off the Lawnmarket and snaked down the steep slope to the Grassmarket and the suburb of Portsburgh. At the other end of the Grassmarket was the West Port, the gate in the city wall used by all traffic entering Edinburgh from the west. Until Victoria Street was opened in 1835, all such traffic making for the High Street, be it the Glasgow mail-coach, a farm cart from West Lothian laden with goods for market, or some distinguished visitor for their Lordships in Parliament House, had to toil up the West Bow, emerging in full view of Mylne's Court.

At the upper end of the West Bow were the city's first Assembly Rooms, where in 1710 a regular programme of dancing was instituted; the arrival of the gentry on Assembly nights must have been a talking-point for Lawnmarket residents. At the lower end of the street, where it joined the Grassmarket, was the spot where most public executions were then carried out, and many a sorry procession from the Tolbooth to the gallows would have brought the inhabitants of Mylne's Court to their windows. One such occasion, in 1736, had a particularly sinister aftermath. John Porteous, the Captain of the Town Guard, had been convicted of the murder of some innocent bystanders after the hanging of Andrew Wilson, a smuggler. On 7 September, a huge crowd gathered in the Grassmarket to witness Porteous' death, only to be deprived of their entertainment by the timeous arrival of a reprieve issued on the instructions of Queen Caroline. That night, however, the incensed city mob broke into the Tolbooth, dragged Porteous out, took him up past Mylne's Court and down the West Bow, and hanged him in the Grassmarket from a dyer's pole. The atmosphere in the streets was tense, and an uncanny silence prevailed as the mob went about its task. The folk in Mylne's Court may merely have been peeping from behind their curtains, but they could not have been unaware of what was going on: perhaps, indeed, it was to their dwelling in Mylne's Court that Mrs Howden the rouping-wife and Miss Grizel Damahoy the seamstress had painfully ascended after the news of Porteous' reprieve earlier in the day, as Sir Walter Scott vividly describes in *Heart of Midlothian.*

Nine years later, the Lawnmarket was the scene of further confusion, when in September 1745 a company of four hundred volunteers was hastily mustered there in a show of resistance against Prince Charles Edward Stuart and his Highland following, then encamped just to the west of the city. The Prince easily gained control of Edinburgh, and in the general disruption which followed Mylne's Court did not escape unscathed. In an attempt to blockade the Castle and starve its garrison out, the Jacobites occupied the key position of the Weigh House: it was at this picket, so one of the stories goes, that there was fired from the Castle's Half-moon Battery the cannon-ball now securely lodged in the wall of Cannonball House, facing the Castle Esplanade. The officers in command of the Weigh House took up residence in the south block of Mylne's Court, in one of the first floor flats occasionally referred to afterwards as 'Prince Charles' Guard Room'. Its owner, Rev. George Logan, was well known for his anti-Stuart pamphleteering activities, and had prudently disappeared for a time, though his supporter and fellow-divine, Alexander Webster, by then resident in Webster's Close in Castlehill, remained on the spot and "displayed a striking proof of his fearless character by employing all his eloquence and influence to retain the people in their loyalty to the House of Hanover".[37] On Logan's return to his dwelling after the Highlanders left Edinburgh on their fatal march to England, he took a somewhat ineffectual revenge by "advertising for the recovery of missing articles abstracted by his compulsory guests".[38]

One further dubious claim to fame possessed by Mylne's Court in the eighteenth century is that it was the home of 'Anderson's pills'. These pills (one illustration shows them as being the size of a walnut) were a particularly strong purgative concocted by a Dr Patrick Anderson who claimed that he was the personal physician to Charles I and that he had obtained the recipe for his 'Grana Angelica' in Venice. These pills were widely known as a popular medicine in Scotland for over two centuries, and it seems that the exclusive right to sell them devolved at some stage upon a resident of Mylne's Court. In 1843 they were still being sold from premises on the second floor of the south block, above the door of which there hung "a decayed portrait of Anderson".[39]

Throughout the eighteenth and nineteenth centuries, Mylne's Court continued to house a wide cross-section of Edinburgh citizens. Though perhaps less popular with the nobility than Mylne's Square, it nevertheless attracted one or two persons of rank, one of the earliest being Sir John Cathcart of Carbiston, who had moved in by 1693. In that year he was deprived of his seat in the Tron Church because Mylne's Court was outwith the Tron's parish, but he successfully petitioned the Town Council to have this seat restored to him on grounds of convenience. The last person of rank to live in the Court was Lady Isabella Douglas, who occupied one of the houses on the west side until 1761. Her family connections show how closely the Scottish nobility was inter-related: one of her grandfathers was the first Duke of Queensberry and the other was the first Marquess of Tweeddale, while her grandmothers were daughters of the first Marquess of Douglas and the first Earl of Buccleuch.

Representatives of the legal profession and the Church were prominent members of the Mylne's Court community through-out the eighteenth century. John Mouat's basement flat was at one time in the possession of Sir David Thoirs, a member of the Faculty of Advocates and a brother-in-law of Lady Isabella Douglas. This same flat was later the property of Andrew Deuchar, Writer to the Signet, who sold it to Rev. John Glen, minister of the second charge at West St Giles from 1733 to 1748. Apart from Rev. George Logan, whose flat was commandeered in 1745, another equally notable city minister, Rev. Patrick Cumming, also had his house in Mylne's Court. Logan was minister of Trinity Kirk from 1732 to 1755, and Moderator of the famous General Assembly of 1740 which deposed Ebenezer Erskine and the Seceders, the first of several dissenting groups which broke away from the Church of Scotland during the eighteenth and early nineteenth centuries. Patrick Cumming held the second charge at the Old Kirk from 1732 until 1737, and from then until 1762 occupied the Chair of Church History at the University of Edinburgh. Three times Moderator of the General Assembly, in 1749, 1752, and 1756, he had a distinguished family: one son, Robert, succeeded him in the Church History chair at Edinburgh, while another, Patrick, was Professor of Oriental Languages in the University of Glasgow for fifty-three years, being appointed in 1761 at the age of twenty.

Stray references to other eighteenth-century residents, such as William Brackenridge, a teacher of mathematics, in 1729, or Mrs Kemp, a teacher of sewing, in 1771, suggest that the humbler professions also had their place, and it would seem that the same social mix as was evident among the first householders of the Court continued for many years. In the first published list of Edinburgh citizens, *Williamson's Directory for 1773-1774*, a variety of legal gentlemen are recorded in Mylne's Court: the sheriff of Inverness, two Writers to the Signet, a solicitor, a procurator, a notary, and three clerks. Interspersed among these are Mrs Frigg, a roomsetter and boarder, James Innes, a surgeon, Thomas Tod, a merchant, Miss Wright, a milliner, and Duncan McMillan, Esq., of Morningside. This directory also records the earliest information available about the owners of the shops at the front of Mylne's Court: two grocers, Robert Herdman and Thomas Livaux, a skinner, David Lindsay, a baker, Benjamin Yule, and the inevitable wine-merchants, Forrests and Maxwell.

The beginning of the nineteenth century, however, brought many changes. The building of the New Town was then well under way, the professional classes and the nobility were moving to it, and the result was the rapid social decline of the Old Town, with tradespeople and commercial premises now constituting the bulk of its population. In 1811, a watch-case maker, Andrew Milligan, was operating from Mylne's Court, and within a dozen years a shoemaker, a weaver, a tobacconist, a silverplater, a clockmaker, a brushmaker, a basket maker, and a candle maker were all plying their trades.

From the 1830s, the annual editions of *The Post Office Directory* give a clear picture of the inhabitants of the Court. In 1834,

Alexander Forbes started business as a master bookbinder, and was to continue operating from the same premises for the next thirty years. In 1839, the Friendly Loan Company is recorded for the first time in the *Directory*: this enterprise was to be associated with Mylne's Court for many years, and its office windows are to be seen on old photographs of the Lawnmarket. In the mid-1830s, a Mrs Wilson ran a lodging-house in the north block, by then known as 5 Mylne's Court,* and elsewhere in the locality there were at least four spirit-dealers, a stationer, and a silver plater. Throughout the 1830s there is mention of tailors and dressmakers operating from Mylne's Court, and the clothing industry in its various forms continued to be carried on during the rest of the century: hatters, boot and shoe manufacturers, strawbonnet workers, stay and stocking makers, shirt makers, and slipper makers are all recorded.

The building was not entirely given up to tradesmen, however. In the south block, 1 Mylne's Court, lived W. J. Lawson, who from 1832 to 1847 held the office of Herald Painter at the Lyon Court. The lawyers lingered on, and for many years the advocate James Grant of Corrimony had his town house in Mylne's Court: son of the Grant of Corrimony who had fought for Prince Charles at Culloden, he was a noted Celtic scholar who published in 1813 his *Thoughts on the Origin and Descent of the Gael*, and on his death in 1835 at the age of ninety-two he was the oldest member of the Faculty of Advocates. In 1836 there is the first mention of Mr M. Pattison, a member of the Society of Solicitors in the Supreme Courts and a Notary Public, who lived at Viewfield Cottage, Morningside but who ran his office from Mylne's Court, situated as it is a convenient distance from Parliament Square and the Court of Session.

With the introduction of more detailed census taking in the middle of the nineteenth century, it is possible to discover the number of people residing in Mylne's Court, together with information about their occupations and status. In 1851, there was the astonishing total of 468 persons living in Mylne's Court: this number was the highest recorded in the nineteenth century, and by 1891 it had fallen to 388. The 1851 figures were perhaps slightly

---

* For the numbering of the houses in Mylne's Court, see fig. 2(ii) (p. 23).

swollen by the presence of a number of lodgers, as at this time there were several lodging houses in the Court, one of the largest being maintained by J. Dickson in no. 1: it had ten lodgers including eight private soldiers, of whom three were recruiting officers and the other five new recruits. The proximity of Mylne's Court to the Castle naturally led to ties between the two, and at various times the Court was the home not only of numerous retired soldiers, who describe themselves as Chelsea Pensioners, but also of wives and families of soldiers still serving in the ranks, and even of serving soldiers themselves: Alexander McIntosh, a sergeant in the 72nd Highlanders, is recorded in the Census for 1861, and ten years later a corporal and a private in the 90th Lowland Infantry were resident in the Court.

The paper industry which had grown up in Edinburgh in the later eighteenth century played a large part in the life of Mylne's Court. Alexander Forbes' bookbindery has already been mentioned, and in 1861 he is noted as having two men, two boys, one woman, and three girls in his employ. It is likely that he recruited his labour force from the immediate neighbourhood, there being many instances of bookbinders and folders, book-sewers, type-founders, and other workers associated with the printing and paper trade amongst the residents of the Court. Later there appear the secondary occupations associated with the paper trade: a paper-bag maker, a venetian blind maker, and an envelope folder were all in Mylne's Court in 1881. The development of printing techniques was no doubt responsible for the replacement of the 1861 "colourist of maps" by the more up-to-date "lithographic worker" of 1891.

Enshrined in the pages of these Census reports are many varied characters whose presence reflects the changing scene in Scottish life as a whole. The saddle-harness maker of 1851 gives way to the railway porter of 1881; the number of Irish residents indicates the extent of immigration, particularly after the severe economic depression in Ireland in the 1840s; the gradual depopulation of the Highlands may be responsible for the resident of no. 5 in 1881 who habitually spoke Gaelic. The maker of surgical instruments, the lamplighter, the maltman, the midwife, even the journeyman painter laconically described as "eccentric": all had their parts to play in the lively kaleidoscope which made up Edinburgh life in the second half of last century. The lowly but respectable trades were represented too, with persons such as the old-clothes man from Ireland, or the washerwoman from Galashiels and her near neighbour and no doubt partner-in-trade the mangle keeper. There were those who followed even more unusual and diverse occupations such as the goldbeater, the die stamper, the fishing rod maker, the tobacco spinner, the tassle and fringe maker, the comb manufacturer, and the umbrella maker. Mylne's Court also housed a family of india rubber workers, and even a truly Dickensian character in the lemonade bottle washer who lived in no. 5 in 1881.

This diversity that was a hallmark of the nineteenth-century inhabitants of Mylne's Court has continued, and is one of the most striking characteristics of its student population today. The residents of the 1980s come from a wide variety of social backgrounds and from all corners of the globe; their studies range widely over most of the subjects offered by the University's eight faculties: and the careers that they will go on to follow will be as diverse as those of their predecessors. The nuclear scientist and the town planner are merely the twentieth-century counterparts of the india rubber worker and the lodging house keeper of earlier days.

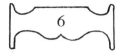

"A GREAT WANT OF FREE AIR":
dilapidation and decline

It has already been stressed that the building of Mylne's Court, Mylne's Square, and the other open courtyards which followed during the early years of the eighteenth century resulted in a great improvement in the living conditions of their inhabitants. However, those fortunate enough to live in such places amounted to only a tiny proportion of Edinburgh's population, and the appearance of these squares could not solve all of the city's problems overnight; indeed, the very fact of their existence probably served to emphasise the desperate plight of those living in the less favoured parts of the town. It is therefore not surprising that the low standards of city life which had doubtless inspired Mylne's reforming zeal in the 1680s continued to decline throughout the eighteenth century.

One of the most obvious problems derived from the well-known Edinburgh custom of disposing of all the household's rubbish and filth by the simple expedient of opening a window and emptying the contents of rubbish-bin and chamber-pot into the street beneath, careless of whoever might be unwise enough to be passing at the time. This practice (claimed by some as the real source of Edinburgh's nickname of 'Auld Reekie') was not only offensive and profoundly unhygienic, but in a city otherwise attractive to tourists had an "evident tendency to discourage others to frequent thereto, or dwell long therein, especially in summer time".[40] Various suggestions were put forward to deal with this problem, including an elaborate set of proposals issued in the 1730s by Robert Mein. This was a subscription self-help scheme, whereby residents in the Lawnmarket, the High Street, and the Canongate would collectively employ two male scavengers to remove the filth daily from each subscriber. Despite obtaining guarantees from a number of residents, including Barbara Scot, whose address is given in the list of subscribers as 'fourth story, Mil's Court' and who with an almost illiterate signature agreed to subscribe two shillings weekly, Mein's scheme seems to have come to nothing. The unsavoury problem persisted (in 1773 Boswell could not prevent Johnson "being assailed by the evening effluvia of Edinburgh")[41] and despite laudable attempts by the Town Council to curb its worst features a permanent improvement in the situation only came about in the 1860s with the appointment of the city's first Medical Officer of Health.

The problem of overcrowding was another which the new courtyards could do little to dispel. The large numbers of children, servants, and apprentices among the first households in Mylne's Court may have prompted the thought that even these spacious new dwellings must have been a little cramped, but the fact remains that these families were immeasurably better off than their neighbours in the narrow closes and wynds elsewhere in the Royal Mile. As urban populations grow, there is a natural tendency for larger living quarters to be subdivided into smaller units, so that what was previously only one family's accommodation comes to provide dwelling-space for several more. In Mylne's Court, this stage in the gradual process of decline began as early as 1708, when Dr Blackadder's brother Adam sold two-thirds of the flat he had inherited, presumably keeping the remaining two rooms for his own use. The same story was repeated up and down the Royal Mile, so that by the middle of the eighteenth century the murmurs of dissatisfaction at the living conditions prevalent in the city had swollen to a flood-tide of complaint and could not be ignored for much longer.

Webster's census of 1755 put the combined population of the old burghs of Edinburgh and Canongate at 36,000. Here was the nub of the problem: too many people living too closely together. The result was, in the words of a far-reaching report of 1752, Sir Gilbert Elliott's *Proposals*, "a great want of free air, light, cleanliness, and every other comfortable accommodation";[42] a particular drawback of the tenement style of building is its common stair, "which is no other in effect than an upright street, constantly dark and dirty"; and of course in such overcrowded and insanitary conditions all kinds of disease were rampant. The only available building space was outwith the city walls, across the Nor'

Loch or south of the Cowgate. The old plan of expansion into these areas, which had been shelved in 1688, was accordingly revived and in 1766 the Corporation announced its famous competition for a design of a 'New Town' to be built on the far side of the Nor' Loch. The following year, the plan submitted by James Craig was accepted, and building commenced soon afterwards. By 1800, first the nobility, and then in close succession the prosperous professional and middle classes, were deserting the tightly packed tenements of the High Street and the Lawnmarket for the elegant Georgian frontages of George Street and St Andrew Square. That Mylne's Court was no exception to the decline which systematically came over the Old Town once the monied classes left is amply illustrated by the changes in the social composition of its residents, as the previous chapter showed.

The building of the New Town, however, was to pose an even more dire threat to the future of Mylne's Court than merely reducing its social status. With the expansion of the city northwards came the need for easier communication between the Old Town and the New. The North Bridge was opened in 1772, but a more westerly link was soon deemed necessary. The credit for making the first move belongs to a Lawnmarket tailor, George Boyd: to shorten the journey between his shop and the new homes of his wealthy customers in Princes Street, he laid a causeway of stones and rubbish across the site of the Nor' Loch, which had been drained in 1762 but was still little better than a swamp. The merits of 'Geordie Boyd's Mud Brig' were immediately obvious, and those engaged in building the New Town began to help it along by depositing there the earth and rubble from their excavations: this they did at first of their own volition, until in 1781 a directive from the Town Council, which had by this time appreciated the sense of Geordie's project, gave them official backing. By 1786, the 'Earthen Mound', as it came to be called, was a substantial embankment broad enough for a group of merrymakers to think of driving a coach-and-six up it. In that year, too, the Town Council began to buy up property in the Lawnmarket with the intention of demolishing it and creating a proper link-road up the slope of the Mound from Princes Street to the Royal Mile. As Mylne's Court lay almost at the top of the Mound, its inhabitants must have wondered what their fate was to be.

Such a grandiose scheme, however, could not hope to survive the economic crises brought on by the French Revolutionary Wars in the 1790s, and the plan was shelved. Not surprisingly — for a link-road up the Mound was an eminently sensible idea — it was revived shortly after the wars ended, and in 1824 the architects William Burn and Thomas Hamilton submitted a scheme which called for the demolition of Mylne's Court and the construction of a road across its site linking the Mound with the Lawnmarket, where there was to be a major road junction, with the new western approach to the city also joining the Royal Mile at this same point. The Improvements Committee of the Town Council, initially hostile to this scheme on the grounds of its cost, was finally won round, but an Improvements Bill incorporating these proposals was rejected by Parliament the following year. The western approach road, now Johnston Terrace, was eventually built more or less as planned, while the problem of linking the Old and New Towns was resolved by continuing the upper end of the Mound round the south of the Bank of Scotland building, a route also proposed by Thomas Hamilton.

Mylne's Court was thus saved from demolition. Had the Improvements Bill been presented to Parliament a few weeks later, however, the result might well have been different, for on 17 April 1825 Mylne's Court fell victim to one of the major hazards of Old Town life: fire. The danger of fire was a constant one, and even with the substitution of stone for wood as a building material expensive and destructive fires happened with alarming regularity: in this, as in so much else, overcrowding was no doubt a major factor. A particularly bad fire in 1725 caused considerable loss of property in the Lawnmarket, and throughout the rest of the eighteenth century reports of further destruction are to be found. 1824 saw two major fires in the Royal Mile, one in June which destroyed five tenements overlooking Parliament Close, and the other in November, "the most disastrous fire recorded in the history of the city",[43] which broke out in the Old Assembly Close and spread quickly to the Cowgate and in the direction of Parliament Square, toppling the steeple of the Tron Church and making over 500 families homeless. The only good to come out of it was that the Town Council felt compelled to purchase "several engines of the newest type", and to organise a standing fire brigade, which, under the command of James Braidwood, was to be the world's first municipal fire brigade. In the following year it was Mylne's Court's turn to suffer, and *The Scotsman's* graphic account of the disaster well illustrates the hazards to which Edinburgh citizens were all too frequently subjected.

Alarming Fire

"Sunday morning between one and two o'clock, a fire broke out in the top flat of a house six stories high in Mylne's Court, Lawnmarket. The alarm which this occasioned was dreadful. It was an old house, surrounded on all sides with buildings of a similar description, and, from the narrow and winding stair, the inhabitants of the burning tenement were able to save very little of their furniture, and some of them had barely time to clothe themselves before they were forced to escape for their lives. The tenants of the adjoining houses were busied all night in removing what they could, and in flying from the scene of danger. The firemen were early on the alert, and notwithstanding the confined nature of the spot, succeeded in bringing three engines to bear upon it. By their exertions the devastation was checked about seven in the morning after the upper three floors were consumed but partly from fire and water, and from falling floors, the whole tenement is in a ruin. .... The engines continued to play on the smouldering ruin till three o'clock on Sunday afternoon."[44]

The new types of fire-fighting equipment were found to be inadequate when confronted with the confined space of the courtyard, but another new invention, Mr Shiell's Triangle (or Tripod), which raised the pipes of the fire engines to make them more effective when dealing with burning buildings of four or five storeys, was used on this occasion for the first time, and helped to confine the damage to the upper storeys of the building.

Fires had a habit of bringing in their train not only physical inconvenience and loss of property, but also social stigma. Rumours immediately arose concerning how and where this fire had started, "mixed with disagreeable insinuations against the occupier of the rooms in which it is said to have originated", and in an attempt to dispel these *The Scotsman* supplemented its report with a letter from one of the residents:

"Sir,

As some surmises have gone abroad prejudicial to one of my fellow sufferers at the late calamitous fire, and which I can distinctly prove to be untrue, I beg leave to do so through the medium of your widely circulated journal. Happening to be among the first, if not the first, to discover the conflagration, I was an eye-witness of the situation in which Mr Bain and family were placed at that time, and shall give a few particulars. Being rather late of getting to bed on the Saturday night, I had scarcely retired to rest, when my daughter observed that she heard a crackling noise, as of wood burning; upon which we immediately got up, and on opening the passage door, were much alarmed to observe flames bursting through the thin wood partition of a door situated between us and the common stair. Rushing past this scene of destruction we awoke Alexander Bain, who, with his wife and child, were asleep in bed at the time, and where in a few minutes more, they must all have perished in the devouring element. I may further state that it was with the utmost difficulty and almost in a state of nudity, that anyone of us escaped from the impending destruction, as, before being discovered, the fire had attained an alarming magnitude. If you think the above statement is in any way calculated to check the insinuations against Mr Bain, its insertion in your columns will satisfy the lovers of truth, by rescuing from unjust imputations the character of a respectable family, and also oblige, Sir, yours etc.,

Isabella Graham"

The steady decline in living conditions in the Old Town, already noted in the eighteenth century, continued throughout the nineteenth, by the middle of which parts of the Royal Mile had degenerated into one of the worst of urban slums: in 1865, for example, the population density of the High Street was 646 persons to the acre. A further unfortunate consequence of the population shift from Old Town to New was that the Old Town no longer contained any citizens of influence or standing: with no spokesman to draw attention to their lot, the inhabitants of the overcrowded and insanitary closes and wynds became a forgotten people. Slum improvement programmes were slow in coming. In 1856, one of the early improvers, Henry Johnston, made a personal inspection of all property in the Royal Mile, and in *A Letter to the Lord Provost, Magistrates, and Council of the City of Edinburgh* he described what he felt should be done to better their condition. Commenting on Mylne's Court and Cranston's Close, he declares: "These might be made very tolerable by drains, paving and whitewash. The entrance into Mylne's Court from the High Street is capacious enough, but it is very narrow and close from the Court into Cranstoun's Close and this should be opened up".[45] At the other side of the courtyard, Mylne's Entry was "very narrow and filthy, covered with human abominations, having therefore a very impure atmosphere"; such closes, Johnston observes, "are unapproachable by any one who is not compelled by necessity to go into them". Similar remarks are made by the census enumerators of 1871, who add the following note to their description of the Enumeration District of Mylne's Court: "A densely populated square with a narrow wynd on both the east and the west sides. Irregularly numbered, very dirty, and anything but a free current of air. In one stair (no. 5), there are 47 families, some of them very numerous. In one house of three rooms (no. 3), on Sunday night there slept fourteen souls of different sexes and no family connections. With all these drawbacks the inhabitants appear healthy and are extremely civil".[46]

With the growth in population and the consequent subdivision of Mylne's large flats, privately owned accommodation in Mylne's Court had long since ceased to be the norm. In the second half of the nineteenth century the principal proprietor was the Free Church, which owned the north and part of the east sides of the courtyard. The members of this church broke away from the Church of Sotland in 1843 and immediately set about acquiring a site for their training college and Assembly Hall. They were fortunate in securing property at the head of the Mound, much of which they then demolished to make way for New College and the adjoining Free High Church and Assembly Hall. In purchasing this property, however, they were obliged also to obtain a number of adjacent buildings, including those in Mylne's Court; where these were not required for the new developments, they were maintained and let, giving the new church an initial annual income of upwards of £150. The Free Church appears to have been a model landlord, and its account books record regular maintenance work: removing rubbish from the cellars, repairing the roof, replacing Mrs Waugh's ball-cock in no. 10 and two of Mr McVie's panes of glass in no. 1, and whitewashing and sizing the stairs of the various tenements in 1878 (at a cost of £2 15s 0d, when the half-yearly rent varied from 17s 6d to £4 7s 11d, depending on the size of the property).

In one respect, however, the Free Church was responsible for the most significant alteration in the appearance of the courtyard since Mylne's day. The Assembly Hall, which had been built on the site of the warren of old houses immediately to the west of Mylne's Court, was too small, and to make room for an extension to it the three quaint old houses which formed the west side of the courtyard were demolished in 1883. Since then, there have been houses on only three sides of Mylne's Court, but it would be wrong to blame the Free Church for thus administering the death-blow to Mylne's concept of a courtyard development, with its four sides focussing on a central square, a separate little community in which all residents would know one another and of which they would all feel part. Such a theoretical concept might work for a generation or two, but seldom survives longer: new residents move in, of whom the old do not approve; the novelty of regarding the inner courtyard as a microcosm of the outer world wears off; and eventually all sense of separate identity is lost. Boswell, who took up residence in neighbouring James Court several decades after its completion, took part in its community life to the extent of becoming a member of its 'Parliament', a society of the inhabitants founded to police the square, but equally he felt no compunction in avoiding his neighbours' company if he so chose. When they organised a ball in February 1776, Boswell absented himself, and instead invited to dinner one of his neighbours, Lord Grange, "he being also a non-conformist".[47] Grange's sentiments on that occasion met with Boswell's full approval: "he said very well that if James's Court were in the middle of a wild moor, its inhabitants must from necessity associate together, but as we are in the middle of a large city, where we can choose our company, it is absurd to be like the inhabitants of a village". It would be surprising if Boswell's contemporaries in Mylne's Court had not held similar views on the breaking up of their own community life; the demolition of Somerville's Land and the adjacent houses was thus perhaps merely the physical culmination of a process which had been going on for many years.

"DIGNITY, SPACIOUSNESS, AND BEAUTY":
the new Mylne's Court

The gradual decline in both social status and physical condition which befell Mylne's Court in the eighteenth and nineteenth centuries was to be dramatically reversed in the second half of the twentieth. In the early years of the present century, however, Mylne's Court found itself involved in one of the most famous and protracted legal cases of the time. As has already been described, much of it had come into the possession of the Free Church, and it formed part of a sizeable complex of Church property at the head of the Mound, including the administrative offices in North Bank Street, the Free High Church, the Assembly Hall, New College, and some houses in Mound Place. In 1900 the Free Church entered into union with the United Presbyterians, forming the United Free Church, which immediately took over all previous Free Church property. A small remnant of the Free Church, however, refused to enter this union, and declaring itself to be the legal successor of the pre-1900 Free Church it claimed all of its property. The competing claims of the two Churches were to exercise the minds of lawyers for almost a decade. In 1904, after an appeal to the House of Lords, the by now much diminished Free Church (whose advocate happened to be the Edward Salvesen after whom one of the Mylne's Court halls was later to be named) was held to be the rightful owner not only of the important group of buildings on the Mound but of churches, manses, and halls throughout Scotland. This decision was totally unworkable, for in practical terms the tiny Free Church was quite incapable of administering the extensive property to which it had fallen heir. Accordingly, a Royal Commission under Lord Elgin was appointed to reconcile the actualities of the situation with the legal position; this led to the Churches (Scotland) Act 1905, which continued the Commission in existence as an executive body charged with the task of assessing the real needs of the two competing Churches and of apportioning the property between them. One of the Commissioners' first duties was to consider the buildings on the Mound, and the outcome of their deliberations was that the offices in North Bank Street were left in the hands of the Free Church, while New College, the Assembly Hall, the Free High Church, and the property in Mound Place were to belong to the United Free Church as from 1 January 1907: these latter properties came into the possession of the re-united Church of Scotland when the U.F. Church joined with it in 1929.

Mylne's Court lay between the Assembly Hall and the North Bank Street offices. Not being used for ecclesiastical purposes, as the other buildings in the area were, it was not hotly contested, and its eventual division between the two Churches seems to have been acceptable to both. To the U.F. Church were allocated the cellars belonging to no. 3, the basement flat on the western side of the north block: these abutted directly on to the Assembly Hall, and came to be used as retiring rooms for ex-Moderators. All the rest of the north block, and most of the east block (i.e. nos. 5, 7, 8, and 10) remained in the hands of the Free Church. Two possible purposes were envisaged for what was by then a set of rather run-down tenements: to provide suitable space for any future expansion of the Free Church headquarters should these outgrow the accommodation in North Bank Street, or to "be remodelled so as to make it more in keeping with modern ideas of artizans' dwellings".[48] In the event, neither of these suggestions was carried out: the North Bank Street building proved more than adequate for both the College and the offices of the Free Church, and the Church had no particular inclination to indulge in property speculation. In fact it now took little interest in Mylne's Court, and apart from sweeping the chimneys free of charge and sending round 'Grey Ladies' to collect the rent, as one former resident recalls, it appears to have done very little to prevent further dilapidation and decay.

Internally, much had changed since Mylne's day. The process of subdividing his spacious flats into smaller units, begun in 1708, had clearly been carried much further by the time of the 1825 fire, and by the beginning of the twentieth century had been taken as far as it could go. In no. 5, the doors on each landing no longer gave access to separate flats: instead, corridors led off to left and right, dark and gloomy passages with squalid rooms opening off them. Over thirty families now lived here, occupying no more than one room apiece. The individual rooms had no water, and a sink on each landing provided a communal supply for the whole floor, while at the end of each corridor was a common toilet whose wooden door had a latch but no lock. Nos. 8 and 10 had suffered a similar fate. Their narrow turnpike stair now gave access to accommodation for three families on each landing, one two-room flat and two single-ends. Here, too, each floor was provided with an outside toilet and a communal sink. In this state the property was to remain until the 1960s.

The remainder of Mylne's Court, nos. 1, 4, and 6, was owned by the City Corporation, who turned out to be rather more forward-looking landlords than the Free Church. A fire in the top floor of no. 6 in 1912 gave rise to some concern about conditions in that part of the building, and most of it was actually demolished some years later, leaving only a single-storey building and a low wall between the two gable ends of no. 4 and no. 8. On the other two stairs lived fifty-two families, mostly in single-ends, and in conditions probably little better than their neighbours across the Court. In 1914-15, however, these blocks were extensively renovated, and were converted into attractive flats for fifteen families, as shown in figure 3(ii). Each floor of no. 4 was turned into one flat, with a room and a kitchen overlooking the Lawnmarket and another room with a window in the gable end looking north. No. 1 had two flats on each floor, one entirely to the front consisting simply of a room and kitchen, and one with one room to the front and a room and kitchen facing the courtyard at the back. A blocked-up doorway still visible on each landing is a relic of this conversion. There were no baths, but each flat had its own toilet. The rooms had coal fires, and there was a big range in each of the kitchens. Lighting was, of course, by gas, the tenants gradually introducing electricity at their own expense. The old 'prayer-cell' windows on the front of the building had earlier been blocked up, but those on the courtyard side were incorporated into the design of the kitchens in the back flats and used as larder windows.

Apart from the strengthening of some of the roof-timbers of nos. 1 and 4 and the rebuilding of the western chimney gable in

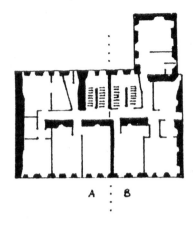

(i) before the City Corporation's renovation of 1914/15: originally two flats (A, B); latterly single-ends

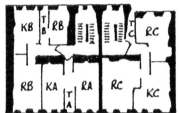

(ii) after the 1914/15 renovation: one 1-room & kitchen flat (A); two 2-room & kitchen flats (B, C)

> R – room
> K – kitchen
> T – toilet

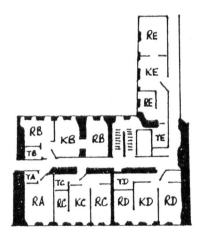

(iii) after the University's renovation of the 1960s: one double room (A); four 2-room & kitchen flats (B-E)

> R – room
> K – kitchen
> T – toilet

Mylne's Court: South Block
upper storeys: three stages of development

FIGURE 3

1937, Mylne's Court underwent no further structural alterations until the 1960s. By then, the pace of deterioration had increased, the north side being very much worse than the south. This was merely a reflection of the continuing decline in living conditions which had affected the area since the mid-eighteenth century, and which had no doubt been greatly accelerated by two world wars and the intervening depression. By the 1950s, much of the Lawnmarket was slum property, and contemporary photographs convey all too vividly the decay and neglect into which this part of it had fallen: grass growing in the courtyard; no windows in the common stairs, allowing rain to blow in and bring dampness to the building; badly dilapidated stonework; roofs that cried out for attention.

Poor living conditions, however, do not necessarily have an adverse effect on the quality of life, and from all accounts the life of the residents of Mylne's Court was a happy one. Outside organisations helped to some extent: early this century the Tolbooth Mission Hall operated from the ground floor of no. 5, with notices in the windows advertising a Mothers' Meeting, a Men's Club, and a Girls' Class. In general, however, it was the residents themselves who kept life going, decorating their window-sills with flower boxes, arranging 'Spitfire Concerts' during the war years to raise money to buy planes, holding courtyard parties for Victory and Coronation celebrations, with tables and chairs supplied by a local bookie, and intriguing the tourists by extending from the kitchen window an old-fashioned washing pulley with an up-to-date television aerial attached to it. In nos. 1 and 4 at least, where the flats were bigger, all the good features of tenement life were to be found: neighbourliness, mutual support, and the blessings of a community where everyone knew everyone else and shared each other's joys and sorrows: even wedding receptions, with all the neighbours invited, were sometimes held within the flats. The children, when not exploring the one large communal bin that stood in the courtyard (and in the process no doubt often falling in), would use the paving stones for peevers or would play endless games of 'chainie' and 'doubler balls'; knowing that there was an easy escape-route over the wall into James Court, they would then go to pester the life out of the various shopkeepers who at different times occupied the line of shops on the ground floor of no. 10: Mrs Smith, the mangle-keeper, who also sold black peas and nuts and vinegar; a sweetie shop; the old Castle Beer Shop; a sweep's store from which soot was sold; a print seller; and a skeechan shop. Skeechan was an intoxicating malt liquor produced during the brewing of ale, which was then mixed with treacle or molasses and sold under somewhat clandestine circumstances as a kind of beer: this shop was open only on Sundays, and claimed to be supplying its customers with nothing more potent than sherbet, as an antidote for the previous night's excesses. If any of the shopkeepers became annoyed with the children, complaints could also be levelled in the opposite direction: one of the early 'lone pipers' at the Tattoo used to practise regularly in the Eagle Bar, the Ensign Ewart's predecessor, until the mothers of Mylne's Court protested that their children were getting no sleep. A clear but unwritten social distinction separated the flats of nos. 1 and 4 from the single-ends of nos. 3, 5, and 7: women might sit and gossip on the steps of no. 5, but this was unheard of on the other side of the courtyard. In wartime, it was different: no. 4 had its own air-raid shelter underneath the pend, but the children preferred to go to the bigger one underneath no. 7, "to have fun with the rest of the gang", as one wartime resident put it.

By the late 1950s the time was fast approaching when something simply had to be done about the state of the north side of the Court. The turnover in tenants had been increasing for some time, and 'to let' notices were frequent sights in the windows. Finally, in 1960 the City Engineer pronounced the building dangerous; it was cleared of its occupants, and the Free Church was warned that it would become the subject of a demolition order in the event of any further deterioration. The Free Church had no use for the property, and could afford neither to put it in order nor to demolish it. By this time, the University of Edinburgh was beginning to express a vague interest in it, and it was suggested in November 1960 that if the Free Church was willing to spend the small sum needed to carry out urgent repairs and stay the City Engineer's hand there was a fair chance that the University would shortly be in a position to buy the property from the Church. The odds were good, but the Free Church was not prepared to gamble. Meanwhile, the Law Society of Scotland, who rented part of the

5 Mylne's Court during reconstruction, 1969: the completed Edward Salvesen Hall is on the left, while on the right work continues on Philip Henman Hall.

6 Edward Salvesen Hall today.

7
Dormers, crow-steps, chimney stacks, and the projecting tower of the turnpike stair make for an attractive roof-line on the east block.

8
The windows on the main staircase of Edward Salvesen Hall. All four have shutters, but only the top pair have glass (see p. 29).

9 The north elevation of Philip Henman Hall: the tiny room in the asymmetrical gable now houses a computer terminal.

Free Church building in North Bank Street, had expressed an interest in acquiring the site: they planned to demolish the building and put up something completely new, with a facade in keeping with its surroundings, but containing modern office accommodation. This plan, however, was overtaken by the pressure of events in those last busy weeks of 1960.

The University's interest in the site had arisen from its current discussions with the Church of Scotland about the future of the Church's property on the Mound. Following on the reunion of the Church of Scotland in 1929, an arrangement had been made between Church and University regarding joint provision of theological education and training for the ministry. This arrangement, whereby the University's Faculty of Divinity was housed in the Church-owned buildings of New College, with the University paying a rent to the Church, was unnecessarily complicated. Moreover, by the late 1950s, New College was badly in need of renovation, and this was naturally a matter of more immediate import to the University than to the Church. Accordingly, a Special Committee had been appointed by the General Assembly of 1959 "to consider the question of the renovation of New College buildings and the advisability of transferring the buildings to the University of Edinburgh".[49] This committee was in the midst of its deliberations when late in 1960 the question mark began to loom over the future of the adjacent part of Mylne's Court. To New College, this was seen as a possible opportunity to extend its library and to create the additional residential facilities that were so badly needed, while the University recognised the wisdom of associating Mylne's Court with New College. Meanwhile, the City Engineer had issued his ultimatum; a decision on whether to repair or to demolish had to be taken within twenty-one days. The Free Church was only too glad to take the easy way out of its dilemma by agreeing to the Church of Scotland's request to convey the property to it free of charge; the Church of Scotland and the University each agreed to contribute £1000 to add to the £5000 promised by the Historic Buildings Council towards the cost of first-aid repairs; and plans for stabilisation were drawn up in ten days and rushed through the Dean of Guild Court. The immediate future of the building was thus assured, but as neither Church nor University had the wherewithal to carry things any further for the moment, it remained in this state for a few years, empty, derelict, but for the time being safe.

In the following year, the General Assembly accepted its Special Committee's conclusion that "it is desirable to convey the New College buildings and the property in Mylne's Court to the University",[50] and although the conveyance was not completed until 1975 the University assumed responsibility for the property as from 11 November 1961. This transfer of property did not, of course, include the Church of Scotland Assembly Hall, which remained the sole property of the Church, along with the ex-Moderators' room in Mylne's Court. This last was to prove a problem in the subsequent redevelopment, and the General Assembly of 1967 agreed to exchange this room for other accommodation elsewhere in the building. The University's intention was to use Mylne's Court as residences for students, and although it was a condition of the transfer that the property be used principally for the benefit of the Faculty of Divinity it was understood that any residential accommodation provided in Mylne's Court would not be restricted to divinity students.

In 1962, discussions began between the University and the City Corporation concerning the future of the south block, which was still inhabited and in somewhat better state, although officially classed as sub-standard. Before long, it too became University property, the gift of the Corporation, who were no doubt delighted at the prospect of someone else restoring it. The University now possessed the whole of Mylne's Court, and began to draw up plans for its conversion. Before anything could be done, however, a considerable amount of money had to be found. It was unlikely that much would be forthcoming from the University Grants Committee, the national body which monitors and partially funds University development: such grandiose schemes were not within its normal ambit. In some ways, the whole undertaking seemed scarcely possible: here was a group of seventeenth-century tenements, some derelict and the rest in sub-standard condition, and the technical difficulties, let alone the cost, of converting them into modern residential accommodation for students seemed well-nigh insurmountable. True, it was an ideal site for a hall of residence, and a restored building pulsing with student life would greatly enhance this part of the Royal Mile, but was the University really aware of what it was taking on?

Fortunately, enough people in sufficiently influential positions were prepared to work towards the realisation of the vision. Sir Michael Swann, who became Principal of the University in 1965, was one of its chief supporters. The architects, Ian G. Lindsay and Partners, were enthusiastic. The Historic Buildings Council, the Pilgrim Trust, and Edinburgh Corporation promised some support. Not until the University received a supremely generous benefaction from Captain Harold Salvesen, however, could the project be launched in earnest and a start made to the restoration of the north and east sides. The University Grants Committee was now persuaded that the scheme was feasible, and agreed to make its normal contribution towards furnishings and professional fees. Work commenced in late 1966, and despite the considerable complexity of the operation, compounded by the difficulty of access to the site, Edward Salvesen Hall was ready to welcome its first residents in January 1969. Meanwhile, an equally generous gift from Mr Philip Henman, an English businessman, enabled the restoration of the south block to begin: work started in no. 1 in 1968, the last residents in no. 4 were rehoused in December of that year, and the first residents in the new Philip Henman Hall arrived in October 1970. The official opening of Edward Salvesen Hall was carried out by His Excellency the Norwegian Ambassador on 5 May 1969, the hall being named after Captain Salvesen's uncle, Edward, Lord Salvesen, the distinguished Scottish judge and conservationist whose grandfather had come to Scotland from Norway in the early nineteenth century: Lord Salvesen's portrait hangs in the common room of the hall, and his crest has been attractively worked into one of its walls. Philip Henman Hall, named after its benefactor, was formally opened by the Earl of Perth, First Crown Estate Commissioner, on 7 December 1970.

An enormous amount of work was involved in the restoration and reconstruction. The main structure was retained, with reinforced concrete floors inserted to stabilise it. The one-storey building surviving on the east side was demolished, and the whole of this side was rebuilt, in matching materials, to the same height as the north side. To construct the boilerhouse and the oil storage tanks, extensive excavations under the courtyard were carried out, involving underpinning the building and cutting through several feet of rock. Mylne's Court is a Category A Listed Building, and therefore changes in its exterior had to be kept to a minimum: the roof, however, was renewed and the chimneys rebuilt, while the opportunity was taken to add a new floor at attic level, throwing out new dormer windows on the north and east sides and inserting additional dormers between the existing ones on the south side. The stonework was entirely cleaned up, and now stands out brightly against the grey frontage of James Court.

Internally, as many significant historic features as could be preserved were retained, some, such as the large stone fireplaces in the corridors of Philip Henman Hall, coming to light again after being covered over during one of the earlier alterations. In other cases, significant features were carefully restored, as described in chapter 3. The distinction between the individual rooms in the north block and the flats in the south block survives: the accommodation in Edward Salvesen Hall consists entirely of single and double study-bedrooms, while that in Philip Henman Hall consists largely of flats, although of a slightly different pattern from previously (see figure 3(iii)). Much else, however, has changed. In Edward Salvesen Hall, each room has its own wash-hand basin, and there is now an ample supply of toilets, showers, and baths. Each flat in Philip Henman Hall has its own bathroom and kitchen unit. Completely new electrical installations were, of course, required, including a new sub-station. A fire alarm system was installed, and two escape staircases built, at the western ends of the north and south blocks. To retain the two entrances and the two internal staircases in the south block would have been an unnecessary waste of space: the entrance to no. 1 now serves the whole of the south block, the dividing wall between its two parts has been breached, and the former stairs of no. 4 provide access to the upper levels. Two lifts have been installed, to suit the convenience of today's less energetic residents.

In the arrangement of the internal accommodation, there is an echo, albeit an unconscious one, of some of the more grandiose recommendations in the influential report of the Committee of Vice-Chancellors and Principals on *The Planning of University Halls of Residence*, published as recently as 1948 but seeming to emanate from a more remote and grander era. "A hall of residence", it advises, "should provide ... a number of common rooms or public rooms of a dignity, spaciousness, and beauty which few students will have had the opportunity of enjoying".[51] This might well describe the split-level common room in Edward Salvesen Hall, or its parquet-floored equivalent in Philip Henman Hall. Several of the other facilities recommended in the report are provided: there is a students' pantry on most levels of Edward Salvesen Hall, while the restored 'Mylne's Room' is now a small study room furnished with an antique oak dining-room table and chairs; the "boot-room" recommended for men students, with "a mechanical boot-cleaner mounted on a rubber block", and the "hairdressing cubicle" for women have, not surprisingly, been omitted; nor is there a room "for listening to the Third Programme on the radio", although the two television rooms are well-patronised. Most fascinating of all, however, are the students' rooms themselves. The authors of the report state that "square rooms should, as far as possible, be avoided: they are difficult to furnish and not very interesting. There should, however, be reasonable variety in shape and size, and in the placing of doors and windows". They could hardly have anticipated such a splendid assortment of rooms as have been devised in Mylne's Court. The unusually shaped rooms are particularly intriguing: the 'banana rooms' in the east wing, tucked cunningly round the curve of the turnpike stair (and to add to the novelty, the floor levels in this part of the building have been altered and one of these rooms has an imposing stone fireplace perched engagingly half way up the wall), and the five split-level rooms on levels 8 and 9 of Edward Salvesen Hall, which utilise the available attic space in a most exciting way. Perhaps it is this variety, more than any other feature, which gives Mylne's Court its unique character and raises it far above the level of a mere institution.

The above description cannot hope to do justice to the ingenuity, imagination, and skill of architects, contractors, and all the variety of consultants involved. The restoration was a massive triumph, and more than vindicated those whose faith in the project had never faltered. The announcement of the Saltire Society's Award for Reconstruction to Ian G. Lindsay and Partners in 1971 is only one indication of the esteem in which the building is held, not least among those who have had the privilege of living in it.

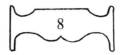

8

"THREE COMMONPLACE LITTLE FLATS":
Patrick Geddes and the development of student accommodation

The conversion of Mylne's historic courtyard into Edward
Salvesen Hall and Philip Henman Hall marked a new stage in the
development of the University of Edinburgh's provision of
residential accommodation for its students. Halls of residence are
now regarded as essential and integral parts of University life, both
by those who live in them and by the University authorities
themselves, who see it as one of their prime duties to their students
to provide an adequate amount of suitable accommodation for
them. It was not always so. With the exception of collegiate
establishments such as Oxford and Cambridge, too different in
character to be really comparable, the British Universities until
fairly recently paid very little heed to their students' living
requirements. The University was a place of learning; for the more
mundane activities such as eating and sleeping, one had to fend for
oneself, sometimes with the help of a motherly landlady, more
often in a cold, damp, uncomfortable, dimly lit garret: a system
which, in the words of one critic, may have "succeeded in
developing self-reliance and independent thought, but certainly
did not make for a well-rounded personality in the university
graduate".[52]

Tentative remarks about the advantages of community life had
gone largely unheeded: as early as 1826, for example, an Edinburgh
student newspaper, commenting on the disjointed nature of the
student body, expressed the view that "if a proper place were
provided, and students not forced, but recommended, to live in it,
and where the holders would be honest and moral, we have little
doubt but that it would tend not only to the prosperity of the
College, but to the ultimate good of the Metropolis".[53] Despite
similar suggestions throughout the century, including the one put

forward in 1884 by Sir Alexander Grant, Principal of the University, for turning George Square into "sets of chambers" for students, the University continued to hold the attitude that where a student lived was his own business. That University policy on student accommodation has so radically changed is very largely the result of a pioneering step taken in 1887, when the colourful and avant-garde thinker, Patrick Geddes, leased three flats in a house at 2 Mound Place, installed seven students, and opened what he called 'University Hall'.

Mound Place dates from the late eighteenth century, an assorted line of houses at the head of the Mound. The only ones surviving are nos. 1 and 2, jointly redesignated no. 4 in 1979; these are substantial dwellings consisting basically of five floors and an attic, although no. 1 virtually loses a floor at ground level due to the steep incline of the street. The remainder of this side of Mound Place, which consisted of the offices of *The Edinburgh Observer* and a large detached dwelling house known as Fox Hall, was demolished in the 1840s to make way for New College. At the end of the eighteenth century, the outlook from these buildings would have been just as spectacular as it is today, although with a very different sort of foreground. Immediately below lay the ugly and in-salubrious clutter of industrial premises known as Tod's Tannery, described once as "the trash of temporary buildings which disfigured the Mound".[54] Beyond this was the site of the Nor' Loch, drained in the early 1760s but still a marshy and unsightly piece of waste ground: Princes Street Gardens were not laid out until the early 1820s. Further off, James Craig's New Town was a-building, but the vast urban sprawl that links the old city with the sea was still in the future. The far view remains unchanged, and unforgettable: the sparkling waters of the Firth of Forth, the green hills of Fife, the fainter line of the Ochils, and, on a clear summer evening, the dim outlines of Ben Vorlich, Ben Ledi, Ben Venue, and perhaps even Ben Lomond away to the north-west.

Such an outlook must have captivated the first residents, thankful no doubt to be quit of their cramped and unpleasant quarters in the Royal Mile or in other parts of the Old Town. Maybe they were not far enough up the social scale to join in the general migration of the upper and middle classes to the New Town; maybe they simply had an understandable reluctance to move so far away from their old haunts, and found in Mound Place a balance between the familiarity of the Old Town and the improved living conditions of the New. At any rate, the early residents of 1 and 2 Mound Place seem to have been largely respectable tradespeople, with a sprinkling of professionals, some of them carrying on their businesses from their homes. In the 1830s and 1840s, for instance, no. 1 housed, among others, a plasterer, an architect, a plumber, a letter-carrier, a merchant, and a currier. From no. 2 there operated the firm of Simpson & Graham, Silver-Platers and Saddlers' Ironmongers, together with a portrait painter, a wine merchant, a coachmaker, a carver and gilder, and a brushmaker; there was also a zinc warehouse, and even a 'Shooting Saloon', opened in 1837 by J. Brand and later taken over as a going concern, first by Thos. Bruce & Co. and then by Crerar & Co. It was no doubt a similar commercial establishment in no. 1 which was responsible for the large shop window which until recently disfigured its frontage.

From 1844, when the Free Church bought up the buildings at the head of the Mound and demolished most of them to make way for New College, the character of the two remaining houses slowly changed. After the College opened in 1850, no. 2 was for some years closely associated with it, the first of several such periods in its history; in it lived both the College janitor, James Kidd, and Dr John Anderson, Lecturer in Natural Science. No. 1 remained more independent, although with less emphasis on commerce among its occupants: a teacher, a sculptor, an artist, a naturalist, and a missionary are all listed in the Post Office Directories for the 1850s and 1860s. In 1877, no. 1 had its first taste of institutionalisation, when it was leased to the Naval and Military Institute and run as a Soldiers' and Sailors' Home; this venture lasted until 1914, when the building reverted to private residential use, and until 1927 part of it was the home of the Warden of New College Settlement. This was an early venture in Home Mission work begun in the Pleasance by New College students in 1876 and organised in 1913 into a Mission Church: the Warden at this time was the Rev. Dr J. Harry Miller, who combined this appointment with the Lectureship in Sociology at New College and who was later to become Principal of St Mary's College, St Andrews.

Ten years after the opening of the Soldiers' and Sailors' Home, a residential development of a much more significant kind took place next door in no. 2, in the form of Patrick Geddes' historic experiment in student accommodation. Geddes' life was one of bewildering complexity and strident unconventionality, spanning the years 1854 to 1932 and covering many parts of the world: lecturer in Botany in Edinburgh and Professor of Sociology in Bombay; town-planner, educationalist, academic *enfant terrible*, biologist, publisher; the organiser of international exhibitions, the founder of summer schools, the master-mind behind the creation of a 'sociological museum' in the Outlook Tower on Castlehill, with its famous Camera Obscura; and the man who conceived the idea of a community of students from different academic disciplines living together and co-operating with one another in managing their environment, only one among his many original ideas that were several decades ahead of his time.

In 1886, Geddes and his newly wed wife had moved into 6 James Court, where he immediately set in motion an imaginative programme of slum improvement among his neighbours. He was then a young lecturer in Botany, and greatly concerned at the conditions in which his students had to live. Accordingly, in nearby Mound Place he leased what he described as "three commonplace little flats, in one of the less unfavourable situations of the dilapidated Old Town".[55] These he redecorated and reorganised to provide accommodation for seven men: study-bedrooms, a common kitchen, a dining-room, and a drawing-room. In May 1887 the first seven students moved in, 'University Hall' was inaugurated, and Scotland had its first student residence. Rents varied from 9/- to 16/- weekly, depending on the extent and type of services requested by the students, while the food costs, reckoned at about 12/- per person weekly, were shared equally. In addition to the advantages the residents would gain from living in close association with students from other walks of life ("that the culture of the Residents may be broadened",[56] as advertisements later proclaim), there would be communicated to them, Geddes hoped, some awareness of the real world outside the ivory tower of the University, through their involvement in his own attempts at urban improvement in the slum areas nearby.

The most striking feature of University Hall to modern eyes was that in its internal affairs it was entirely self-governing. In evidence laid before the Scottish Universities Commission in 1891, Geddes described how

"the residents lost none of that independence which rightly is an old and cherished tradition in Scotland. Instead of having University Hall administered by wardens or masters, the students themselves assume full control of the internal management of the houses. They decide who may be a resident, what the rules of conduct shall be and how enforced; they take turns in supervising the domestic staff which prepares meals and cares for the rooms; and finally, after dividing the actual cost of rent and provisions among their number, they live more comfortably and more cheaply than is possible anywhere else in Edinburgh."[57]

Those familiar with the complex business of running a modern hall of residence will shudder at this recipe for chaos, especially when it is realised that the committee of residents which managed the internal affairs of the hall was elected on a monthly basis. The arrangement seemed to work, however, at least to begin with, and the first residents placed on record "their sense of the pleasure and profit of their mutual intercourse, and their conviction of the benefits to be derived from the system".[58] The social side of life in University Hall also went well: by 1889, with increasing numbers of students, it had both a tennis club and a boating club, to be followed shortly by clubs for cricket, football, golf, fencing, and swimming; there were societies for, *inter alia*, biology, geography, Celtic, dramatics, and 'applied ethics and social science'; and there are several references in contemporary student magazines to the vigorous nature of the University Hall 'Smokers'.

University Hall was independent in another way: neither the University nor the city authorities were at all enthusiastic towards it. Members of the University staff served from the beginning on the external Committee of Management, but they did so in a private capacity. Later, when Geddes' energies in extending his various enterprises outran his business capabilities, they were taken over not by the University but by a private association, the Town and Gown Association, Ltd., launched in May 1896. Its name reflects Geddes' ideal of close co-operation between city and university, an ideal expressed also in its motto, *Floreat Res Publica, Vivat Academia,* borrowed from the old student song, *Gaudeamus Igitur.* A stock-holding company whose directors represented the business and academic life of the capital, its principal purpose was to manage University Hall and so relieve Geddes of the burden of administering the various properties for which he was legally responsible. This it continued to do until the 1930s, when financial difficulties forced the Association to dispose of its various properties one by one.

By 1896, the running of University Hall had become well-nigh a full-time job, for it had, of course, proved an immediate and resounding success. The whole of 2 Mound Place was taken over in 1888 and a further thirteen students were accommodated. Part of Riddle's Court in the Lawnmarket was acquired in 1891. Next Geddes bought up property in Ramsay Garden, including the octagonal 'goose-pie lodge' built for the poet Allan Ramsay in 1740: in the autumn of 1893 this became the headquarters of University Hall, and was to remain so throughout the rest of its history. The greatest single development, however, was the opening in April 1894 of the new and imposing extension to Ramsay Lodge, adjoining the Castle Esplanade. From its humble beginnings with seven students, University Hall now had 120 residents in several different houses: as a contemporary eulogist put it, "Since Amphion raised the walls of Thebes by his music, there has been nothing like the raising of University Hall by the eloquence of Patrick Geddes".[59] Equally flattering was Sidney Webb's remark on a visit to Ramsay Lodge: "Geddes, you are making a northern Balliol".[60]

The principle of self-government was maintained, each house having its own separate internal committee, with the external affairs of the whole organisation controlled by the Town and Gown Association. The complete absence of any kind of internal authority had, however, proved something of a problem, and members of the University staff were soon given positions of a mildly supervisory nature within each house: by 1894 the publicity material was announcing that "young students can be placed under the care of one of the resident tutors".[61] This was nevertheless not allowed to obscure Geddes' basic principle of self-government, and when in 1912 a great debate was raging over the respective merits of halls with wardens and halls without, a group of nine ex-residents of University Hall looked nostalgically back to their student days and stated their views very firmly:

"We must frankly confess our dread of a type of residential hostel which is already beginning to arise, where authority may take the reins without giving self-control a chance, and where a too great uniformity threatens to take the place of that mêlée of heterogeneous but congenial spirits which was one of the charms of University Hall when we knew it many years ago."[62]

Not only was University Hall a success in itself, but almost immediately Geddes' ideas began to bear fruit in a number of other quarters. In 1894 the 'Crudelius University Hall for Lady Students' was opened in Burns' Land, 457 Lawnmarket; in 1895 'The Church of Scotland Residence for Divinity Students in the University of Edinburgh and Probationers' came into being at 14 George Square; and in 1897, under the auspices of the Edinburgh Association for the University Education of Women, Masson Hall was founded in premises at 31 George Square. More significantly, the University itself had at last been alerted to its responsibilities and had been forced to acknowledge the wisdom of Geddes' activities. From the foundation of University Hall, the University had given it a brief mention in its annual *Calendar*, listing it among the 'University Societies and Clubs', where it was sandwiched between the 'Total Abstinence Society' and the 'White Cross Society' (whose object was "to form a healthy public opinion amongst the students of this University on the subject of Personal and Social Purity":[63] Geddes would have approved). In 1898, however, there appears a new section in the *Calendar* entitled 'Residences and Board for Students', listing University Hall, Crudelius House (as it had come to be called), Masson Hall, and the new Muir Hall for female medical students at 12 George Square. Halls of residence were now regarded as sufficiently respectable and permanent parts of University life to be placed in a category of their own, distinct from the multitude of student societies which blossom one year only to wither the next. This was a tacit admission on the part of the University of the need to provide student accommodation, although it was not until 1918 that official

University accommodation came into being, when the management of Muir Hall was transferred from a private company to the University Court: Masson Hall came similarly under the University's aegis in 1919. The final stage in this process came in 1929, when Cowan House was opened in George Square, the first hall actually to be established by the University.

That Geddes was indirectly responsible on a different level for the University's change of policy is illustrated by the story of how Cecil Rhodes had been persuaded by Geddes to consider Edinburgh as well as Oxford as a suitable recipient for his benefactions. When Rhodes began to make enquiries about the University in the late 1890s, he was surprised to discover that it provided no residential accommodation for its students, and even more surprised to hear that it had refused to have anything to do with University Hall. This unenlightened attitude struck Rhodes so forcefully that he removed Edinburgh's name from his deed of benefaction, leaving Oxford as the sole host for his Rhodes Scholars. The chagrin of the University Court on learning this must have made them realise that there was something in what Geddes was doing after all. Further acknowledgement of the value of Geddes' pioneering work was made in 1954 by Sir Edward Appleton, then Principal and Vice-Chancellor of the University; speaking during a celebration of the centenary of Geddes' birth, he indicated that the University was intending to increase its stock of student accommodation (an intention that was shortly to be fulfilled in the building of the Pollock Halls) and admitted that Geddes had revealed a need which "has certainly been one of the factors influencing our subsequent policy".[64]

When the focal point of University Hall moved to Ramsay Garden and Ramsay Lodge in 1894, Geddes did not renew the lease on 2 Mound Place. The Free Church decided to use the property itself as a residence for its students, and the building's previous association with New College was resumed. It was now known as the Free Church College Residence or, from 1900, New College Residence: in that year, on the union of the Free Church with the United Presbyterians, New College and all adjacent property had come into the possession of the new United Free Church. For some unrecorded reason, this attempt to create a College residence was a complete failure, and in 1903 the U.F.

Church gladly leased the building again to the Town and Gown Association.

University Hall was still expanding, and by now included St Giles' House at 22 St Giles Street, Blackie House in Wardrop's Court, and property in James Court. Even more accommodation was required, and when 2 Mound Place was taken over again in 1903 it was further altered internally to provide rooms for a total of thirty students. The stonework around the front door still bears the dates 1887 and 1903, marking the beginnings of Geddes' two periods of association with the building. At this time, too, it was rechristened Lister House, in honour of Lord Lister, the illustrious Professor Emeritus of Surgery. Geddes had a great admiration for Lister, and included a portrait of him in the series of 'Pictures of imagination, of magic, and romance' which he commissioned from John Duncan, R.S.A. for the Common Room of Ramsay Lodge. This series of paintings, which includes such diverse characters as Cuchullin, St Mungo, the Admirable Crichton, and John Napier of Merchiston, illustrates the theme that "wherever a man learns power over Nature, there is magic; wherever he carries out an ideal into Life, there is Romance".[65] In including Lister, the pioneer of antiseptic surgery, Geddes questioned "whether any single individual has ever rendered a greater service to humanity".

Lister House continued to be part of University Hall until 1914, when the activities of the Town and Gown Association began to contract and the lease was not renewed. New College again took over, and ran it as a student residence until 1920. From then until 1952 Lister House was a hostel for women students, managed successively by St Margaret's Club, the Church of Scotland Woman's Guild, and the Church of Scotland Committee on Social Service.

During this period, in 1927, part of 1 Mound Place became incorporated in Lister House. In that year, no. 1 was divided into two parts. On the three upper floors, the thick party walls separating nos. 1 and 2 were pierced, and Lister House spilled over into these three floors; with the extra accommodation now available it could house fifty-one female students and a resident staff of six. The two lower floors of no. 1 were leased to the Scottish Girls' Friendly Society. This had originally been founded as a kind of welfare club for country girls working as maidservants in big houses in the city, but was by then also providing residential accommodation for girls working in factories and shops, and from 1927 until the early 1960s it ran the Alexandra Hostel for Working Girls in the ground and first floors of 1 Mound Place. The ground floor contained a sitting-room and a dining-room, a kitchen, and staff accommodation. Upstairs were six bedrooms, several for three or four girls each. In all, seventeen girls and one resident member of staff occupied the two floors.

Early in 1952 Lister House was closed down. The electric wiring was in a parlous state, the floors were sagging, there was dampness throughout the building, and the Committee on Social Service could not afford the cost of rehabilitation. New College, now owned by the Church of Scotland as a consequence of its union in 1929 with the U.F. Church, again seized its opportunity, as it had done in 1894 and in 1914. For some years, the College had hoped that either Lister House itself or the ground on which it stood might at some stage be used for an extension of its own facilities. In 1934, conscious of increased pressure on space in the Old Library caused by large accessions at the time of the 1929 union, the Senatus of New College considered Lister House as a possible new location for the Library: a plan was drawn up for a completely new building to house 200,000 volumes, but its estimated cost of £40,000 was too high and the alternative site of the Free High Church, which was by then closed, was chosen instead. Later in the 1930s another plan was conceived to demolish the existing building and erect a College Chapel and a new residence for students, but in the difficult years of the war and its aftermath this plan had been allowed to lapse.

Now, however, an opportunity for extension was again presenting itself. The only residential accommodation possessed by New College was a pair of adjacent houses at 22 and 24 Chalmers Street, the successor to the Divinity Students' Residence established in 1895 in George Square. These houses held only twenty-two students, and were quite inadequate for the post-war needs of the College. Fortunately, the obvious solution commended itself to all parties: management of Lister House was transferred from the Committee on Social Service to New College, the Chalmers Street residence was sold, and the proceeds of the sale went towards the restoration of Lister House.

The restoration required was extensive. In addition to re-inforcing the floors and upgrading the electrical installations to meet the more stringent fire regulations of the day, the opportunity was taken to replace the old open coal fires with a new low pressure hot water system fired by a boiler installed in the basement. Other structural repairs were carried out: a connecting passage with the College itself was provided (later to be closed off when New College was internally restructured in the 1970s), and a corridor was driven through the party wall separating Lister House from the Alexandra Hostel on the two lower floors, to create an emergency escape route. The architect also recommended the complete renewal of certain floors "in view of the fact that the building is to be occupied by male students instead of female" and the estimate for this part of the contract was promptly trebled!

All this was to cost a vast amount, and the sale of the Chalmers Street hostel could not of itself be expected to raise sufficient money. Other sources had to be found: New College Settlement in the Pleasance was sold about this time, and the income was partly used for Lister House; a number of generous gifts and legacies was received (including a very substantial contribution from the Rev. Dr John Somerled Macdonald, a former student of the College who had emigrated to the United States; his name was given to the room in which the library was later housed): and there was an appeal to various charitable bodies, although with only moderate success — when pressed as to the building's claims to architectural or historic merit, Principal Baillie of New College had to admit that Lister House "might be said to be quaint and characteristic rather than beautiful in its external appearance".[66] Drawing on these various sources of finance, the total cost of £16,616 7s 0d was eventually met.

On 1 August 1954 the Matron, staff, and furniture from Chalmers Street were moved to Lister House, and the building entered upon the next stage of its existence, under the revived name of New College Residence. The official opening ceremony was performed by Sir Edward Appleton on 7 October 1954. Between forty and fifty divinity students were accommodated, in single and double study-bedrooms. On the ground floor were the kitchen and dining-room, and on the first floor was a large common room; some accommodation was also provided for resident staff on the first and second floors. The Residence was managed by the Senatus of New College, with the day-to-day running in the hands of a Warden, who was sometimes a member of staff of the College and sometimes an older student, sometimes resident and sometimes non-resident, a Senior Student, who acted as the Warden's deputy, and a Matron. From all accounts, it was a happy place, and many ministers throughout Scotland, and indeed throughout the world, look back on their student days in New College Residence with affection.

In its internal organisation, New College Residence was to continue virtually unchanged until 1973, although important developments in its relationship with the outside world had by then taken place. As explained in the previous chapter, the University of Edinburgh took over from the Church of Scotland in 1961 responsibility for the site and buildings of New College. It seemed only logical that the adjacent Residence should follow suit, as it too had much closer ties in practice with the University than with the Church, but it was not until 1964 that it became University property, and on this occasion the University had to pay for its new acquisition. Technically, New College Residence was now part of the University's general stock of student accommodation, and was no longer restricted to divinity students, but its proximity to New College naturally meant that for a few years at least they remained in the majority. By this time, too, the University had acquired Mylne's Court, and its conversion into a new complex of halls of residence was soon to begin. It seemed sensible to link New College Residence with the new halls, and on the opening of Edward Salvesen Hall in January 1969 the Residence somewhat reluctantly surrendered its independence and joined this larger grouping, retaining its Matron and its Senior Student, but now operating under the general oversight of the Warden and Domestic Bursar of Mylne's Court.

The Alexandra Hostel, in the ground and first floors of no. 1, had closed in the early 1960s, largely because there was no longer any real demand for this kind of residential accommodation. At the time, the Senatus of New College suggested that it might be converted into flats for the College caretaker and the domestic staff of the Residence, with a bicycle shed, a laundry, and a table-tennis room in the basement, but the cost of the proposed alterations, given the general state of the property, made this proposal impracticable, and this part of the building remained empty for a number of years. The truth was that, despite the structural alterations of the 1950s, the whole building was not in a sound state. In 1973, the University's architect reported that shrinkage of the clay sub-soil beneath the foundations was producing settlement, with a differential settlement between the external and the internal walls; in addition, the west gable, into which tell-tales had been built some years previously, was moving and disintegrating. In that state, the building's days were numbered, and in the summer of 1973 New College Residence was closed, after an anxious few months when structural checks were carried out at frequent intervals as a precaution against possible further deterioration. Already in 1961 a Church report had stated that "as the building is of traditional Scottish tenement construction and has required strengthening on several occasions, its life must be considered as very limited and the site only of value for possible future extensions".[67] The site was indeed of value, for the Faculty of Divinity was expanding to such an extent that New College was barely large enough to cope with the increased numbers of students. The plans of the 1930s were therefore revived: New College Residence and the neighbouring buildings in Ramsay Lane were to be demolished and replaced by a new student residence, a College chapel, and additional teaching rooms. The project was an attractive one, but there was also considerable pressure to preserve existing buildings. An appeal for funds failed to raise the necessary finance, and by the mid-1970s it had become clear that such an elaborate scheme was no longer likely to be implemented within the foreseeable future. Accordingly, the Residence was given a new lease of life: by the end of 1975 plans for its conservation and renovation were being discussed, and in October 1978 it again opened its doors to students, under its new name of Patrick Geddes Hall.

Again, a vast amount of work had to be done, and the University was fortunate in receiving assistance from the Carnegie Trust, the Historic Buildings Council, the Pilgrim Trust, and Edinburgh District Council in meeting the total cost of approximately £330,000; it was fortunate, too, in again securing the services of Ian G. Lindsay and Partners as architects. The biggest problem was caused by the sagging floors: these have now been keyed in to steel beams, inserted as a framework into the building with immense care and precision: the floors still sag, as a quaint reminder of their past, but they now do so in safety. The coal-fired boiler has been removed, and an entirely new heating system connected up with the boilerhouse in Mylne's Court has been installed. The building has been rewired throughout, and ever stricter fire regulations have necessitated a complete new emergency alarm system with smoke detectors. The lower floors of no. 1, unoccupied since the closure of the Alexandra Hostel, have at last been incorporated into the rest of the building, so that for the first time the two houses form a single unit. The ugly Victorian shop window which disfigured the frontage of the hostel has been replaced by three ordinary windows in keeping with those in the rest of the building, while all other windows which had lost their Georgian astragals have had these replaced. Internally, all rooms have been completely redecorated and refurnished, but cornices, moulded ceilings, panelling, bottle glass windows, decorative curved cupboards, and other original features that have survived previous alterations have been retained where possible. On the ground floor, a laundry room and a common room have taken the place of the old kitchen and dining-room, no longer required as such now that the Rainy Hall provides dining facilities for the whole of the Mylne's Court complex. The upper floors contain thirty double and seventeen single bedrooms, all newly provided with wash-hand basins; on each floor there is also a small pantry where tea or coffee can be made.

Patrick Geddes Hall was formally opened on 10 November 1978 by H.R.H. the Duke of Edinburgh, Chancellor of the University, who unveiled a plaque commemorating the building's historical importance. Much has happened to these old Georgian houses during the past century, but as their present occupants look out over the city and watch the haar come rolling in from the Forth, or gaze enraptured at a summer sunset behind the Highland Line, they are in a very real sense the spiritual descendants of those seven students who shared Patrick Geddes' great adventure of 1887, and who set a pattern of community living for which several generations of their successors, here and elsewhere, have had much cause to be thankful.

9

"A COMPREHENSIVE SCHEME OF LONG STANDING":
the Mound/Lawnmarket area

"A comprehensive scheme of long standing" was how Patrick Geddes described in 1915 his plans for the Old Town of Edinburgh, "the preservation and renaissance of historic Edinburgh, from the standpoints both of town and gown".[68] His dream has not been fully realised, but in the area between the Mound and the Lawnmarket it has perhaps come closest to being so. Now part of one of the city's official Conservation Areas, the Mound/Lawnmarket area contains a number of University properties and in November 1966 the University and the city began to co-operate with plans for its development and conservation. Thanks to the vision of men like the Very Rev. Professor John McIntyre, Principal of New College from 1968 to 1973 and Principal Warden of the University's Halls of Residence from 1960 to 1971, backed up by the skill and determination of the staff of the University's Buildings Office and the expertise of its architects, much has been achieved. The rehabilitation of Mylne's Court and Patrick Geddes Hall has benefited both city and University, contributing immeasurably to the amenities of the former and to the facilities of the latter. In this context, the other buildings in this area with University associations are likewise of interest, especially as in many cases their history impinges upon that of Mylne's Court.

James Court

One of the first persons to copy Robert Mylne in his pro-gramme of urban development was James Brownhill. Immedi-ately to the east of Mylne's Court he built a somewhat larger courtyard in the 1720s, called in his honour James Court (b).*

---

* Letters in parentheses refer to the plan of the Mound/Lawnmarket area shown in figure 4.

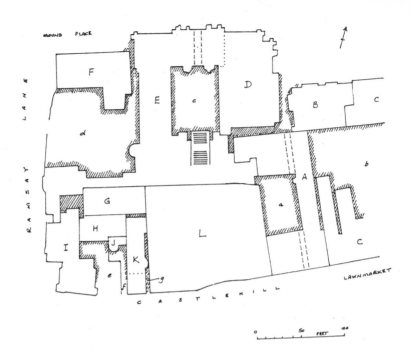

BUILDINGS

A Mylne's Court
B Free Church Offices
C James Court
D New College Library
   (formerly Free High Church)
E New College
F Patrick Geddes Hall
G Rainy Hall
H Rainy Hall Kitchen
I Outlook Tower
J Sempill's House
K Sempill's Close
L Assembly Hall

OPEN SPACES

a Mylne's Court
b James Court
c New College courtyard
d New College garden
e Rainy Hall kitchen yard
f Sempill's Close
g Jollie's Close

The Mound-Lawnmarket area, 1983

FIGURE 4

When the University became interested in Mylne's Court, it also began to acquire parts of James Court, particularly nos. 3-7 on the south side and no. 6 on the north, the part in which Patrick Geddes was living when he founded University Hall in 1887. It was hoped that finance might eventually be found to include James Court in the new complex of halls next door; the boilerhouse in Mylne's Court was made of sufficient size to cope with an additional load, and an underground link was planned between the common room in Philip Henman Hall and James Court. Unfortunately, increasing deterioration in the state of the property, together with the economic difficulties of the 1970s, caused this ambitious scheme to be abandoned, and the University has surrendered its interest in James Court. Happily, however, parts of it have now been privately developed and nos. 3-7 leased back to the University for use as student flats.

New College

From their position on the ridge high above the Nor' Loch, the first residents of Mylne's Court enjoyed the same open northward view as was to attract the first residents of Mound Place a century later. Nothing of any substance lay immediately to the north: a cluster of stables and haylofts was all that occupied the sloping ground at the foot of Cranston's Close, perched on the edge of the steeper decline that ran down into the loch below. The Town Councils of the seventeenth and eighteenth centuries had ambivalent feelings about this loch. Its presence was useful as a ducking-pond for evil-doers, as an eel-fishery, and, more importantly, as a defence, for the Flodden Wall did not completely surround the city, the loch being regarded as a sufficient barrier on the north. The likelihood of an English invasion was now very remote, but it was still desirable to have some means of stopping others who might wish to make their way clandestinely into the city, particularly smugglers from the ports of Leith and Granton. There was, however, one major disadvantage, in that the loch was too convenient as a dumping-ground for the city's rubbish. Accordingly, as first one view and then the other prevailed, the loch was drained and then allowed to refill on several occasions between 1663 and 1762, in which year the city's expansion to the north was finally seen as inevitable, and the balance was swung in favour of permanently draining it.

In 1757 Rev. Patrick Cumming, previously noted as occupying one of the flats in Mylne's Court, built a three-storey dwelling house on the vacant ground to the north of the Court, which later became the home for a few years of Robert Murray, Receiver General of H.M. Customs in Scotland, and eventually was to house the offices of *The Edinburgh Observer*. In the 1840s this building and all the surrounding ground at the head of the Mound was bought by the Free Church, which had come into being as a result of the Disruption of 1843, and with commendable zeal had been quick to raise sufficient money to acquire this imposing site for its principal buildings. These buildings still stand, an impressive group well worthy of their site, largely the work of the eminent architect W. H. Playfair. Chief among them is New College (E), one of the three training colleges for ministers which the Free Church built throughout Scotland: its foundation stone was laid in 1846, and the College was opened on 6 November 1850. Sharing its site, and contributing to the group's splendid skyline, is the Free High Church (D), now New College Library. Behind these, and fronting the Lawnmarket, is the Assembly Hall (L), where the annual meetings of the General Assembly, the Church's highest court, are held. This was designed by David Bryce and opened in 1859; it was extended into Mylne's Court in 1885, occasioning the demolition of the three old houses on the west side of the Court. Chapter 7 explained how all this property was transferred first to the United Free Church and then, in 1929, to the reunited Church of Scotland, and also how New College came to be associated after that date with the University of Edinburgh: it continues to house the University's Faculty of Divinity, while also functioning as one of the Church of Scotland's four training colleges.

The Rainy Hall

One section of New College has come to be so closely associated with Mylne's Court that it is now regarded as an integral part of the residential complex: the Rainy Hall (G). "Dining, as distinct from feeding, is a social function which deserves, even demands, dignified surroundings",[69] pronounced the 1948 report on *The Planning of University Halls of Residence*. Few halls opened in the

1960s can boast that they have fulfilled that dictum as successfully as Mylne's Court has done, albeit accidentally, for in the Rainy Hall it possesses a quite unusually splendid dining hall.

The Rainy Hall was built on the site of the former Moncrieff Hall as part of a major internal reorganisation of New College carried out to celebrate its golden jubilee, and was opened on 2 November 1900 amid the euphoria which accompanied the first General Assembly of the new United Free Church, which had come into being only three days previously. The hall was named after Principal Robert Rainy (1826-1906); he had been minister first in Huntly and then in the Free High Church, Edinburgh, before succeeding to the Chair of Church History at New College in 1862, coupling this post with that of Principal of the College from 1874. One of the most distinguished ministers of the Free Church (he had been Moderator of its General Assembly in 1887), Principal Rainy was largely responsible for guiding it towards union with the United Presbyterian Church, and on the resulting formation of the United Free Church in 1900 he was called to be Moderator of its first General Assembly, an office which he held again in 1905. In the legal tussle over ownership of property which followed this union, described briefly in chapter 7, it was Rainy who staunchly upheld the claims of the U.F. Church against the case put up by the remnant of the Free Church which had not come into the union.

The hall was the work of Sidney Mitchell, a less well-known figure than either Playfair or Bryce but nonetheless an architect with some notable buildings to his credit, such as the Well Court in the Dean Village and the University Union in Teviot Place. It possesses much of the ambience of a medieval Oxbridge college hall. The lower parts of the walls are panelled with light oak, surrounded by a decorative frieze, while a carved stone surround lends distinction to the arched doorways. The upper parts of the walls originally provided hanging space for some of the Church's large collection of portraits of distinguished ecclesiastics, who gazed solemnly down upon the antics of their successors below: when the Church conveyed the Rainy Hall to the University in 1961, these portraits were removed, and a landscape of Iona is now the only painting. Ornamental pendant lamps hang from the ceiling, which is elaborately decorated with sombre browns, reds, and greens; its massive supporting beams rest on ornately carved and gilded braces. On the west wall, a large bronze medallion of Principal Rainy gives the hall a focal point: this is the work of a Belgian sculptor, Paul Wissaert, who found himself stranded in Edinburgh on the outbreak of war in 1914. He was befriended by Dr Alexander Whyte, Principal of New College from 1909 to 1918, who was instrumental in raising subscriptions to enable the medallion to be executed: a copy is in Rainy's first church in Huntly.

Perhaps the most intriguing feature of the hall is the collection of 157 transfers of heraldic shields which decorate the top of the panelling around the walls. These represent a wide variety of persons and institutions. The Church's emblem, the Burning Bush, recurs at regular intervals on the side walls, while flanking the Rainy medallion are the shields of Glasgow, Aberdeen, and Edinburgh Universities, the three universities which had Free Church colleges associated with them: the Edinburgh arms appear in an unusual form, the shield being divided by a chevron instead of the normal saltire. Scotland, England, and the cities of Aberdeen, Edinburgh, and Glasgow are all represented, along with Bishop Wardlaw (the founder of the University of St Andrews, appearing here in a most unepiscopal setting) and Sir Thomas Hope, the distinguished seventeenth-century Lord Advocate. The vast majority of the shields, however, are those of Scottish noble families. The heads of no less than fifty-six families are represented, Earls, Barons, and others of lesser rank, these last having their shields surmounted by a thistle motif in place of the customary coronet. Several of these noble houses count eminent churchmen among their members, but there seems no reason for this particular selection to have been made and no significance in their largely random arrangement around the hall. As a decorative feature, however, these heraldic devices could hardly be bettered.

Initially, the Rainy Hall's main function was to serve as a dining hall for New College, and it was provided with a small kitchen entered by a door in the south wall. It was also regularly used for major lectures, meetings, evening classes, and social events. In 1936 the Free High Church was converted into a new library for the College, and the old library, renamed the Martin Hall, became another attractive venue for lectures and meetings. The Rainy Hall was now underused, and when the expansion of residential facilities in the Mound/Lawnmarket area was being planned in the 1960s it seemed sensible for the students in the new halls to eat in the Rainy Hall as well as those from New College. This greatly increased use necessitated a completely new and much enlarged kitchen (H), and a second doorway was knocked through the south wall of the hall, with a new carved stone surround to match the existing one. Long refectory tables and benches were specially made, adding to the collegiate atmosphere of the hall.

The kitchen produces well over 3000 meals per week in the height of term. Mylne's Court residents are given breakfast and dinner daily, with lunch in addition at weekends. Students and staff of New College are provided with morning coffee — one of the great social events of the day — and a snack lunch. There are the grander moments too: the Christmas meals, when the hall looks its best, with polished glassware reflecting the candlelight and a Christmas tree brightening up one corner; the Burns Suppers, when the haggis is duly piped in to the bewilderment of overseas residents; and the occasional formal dinner. On an informal level, social events such as ceilidhs, dances, and discos are established features in the calendars of both Court and College.

The Rainy Hall's proximity to the Assembly Hall has led to its use as ancillary accommodation for the latter. Part of it, for example, has been used at the time of the General Assembly to house its bookstall. A more colourful role which the Rainy Hall was formerly called upon to play was in connection with Edinburgh Festival productions in the Assembly Hall. Each year from 1948 to 1969 the actors used the Rainy Hall as additional backstage accommodation. Wooden partitions were erected to create makeshift dressing rooms, and there are memories of water-boys running around filling pails of hot water into the zinc baths which had to serve the actors in place of showers. Sometimes, too, the company used the Rainy Hall as a place of rehearsal until the stage was erected in the Assembly Hall. Not a few famous names in the theatrical world have waited here for their cues. When the Old Vic played 'Hamlet' in 1954, one of the actors, making one of his first major performances, was the young Richard Burton. Sir Laurence Olivier and his wife appeared in 'St Joan' in 1963. 'Oh, What a Lovely War!' had its beginnings in the Rainy Hall, when its originators were appearing in another Assembly Hall production and began discussing their next venture. With the opening of Edward Salvesen Hall in 1969, however, the Rainy Hall was required throughout the summer for the provision of meals to conference visitors and ceased to be available for theatrical purposes.

Ramsay Lane

The space between the Rainy Hall and Patrick Geddes Hall was formerly known as the Garden Court of New College (d). The garden sits well to the sun, and its mature trees make it a pleasant and shady spot in summer. It once housed a telescope, and was originally enclosed on all four sides, the west side being formed by a line of dilapidated buildings that had at one time been stables. These were demolished in the early 1970s when New College's plans for expansion on this site still seemed feasible. The subsequent shelving of these plans has resulted in the garden being now open to the west: it has been completely relandscaped, with a new stairway providing an emergency escape route from Patrick Geddes Hall to Ramsay Lane. The fine stone wall separating the garden from Ramsay Lane was constructed in 1978. It includes a stone with the date 1637 and the letters 'HIV': future historians will no doubt contrive to find a variety of explanations for its presence here. The truth is that this is simply a piece of architectural bravado: the stone has no connection with this site, and was donated by a local resident who was anxious that it should be put to good use.

The two remaining buildings further up this side of Ramsay Lane have no connection with Mylne's Court. First comes the Ramsay Lane wing of New College, opened in 1837 as the Tolbooth Parish School and taken over ten years later by the great Free Kirk minister, Dr Thomas Guthrie, who founded here his 'Edinburgh Original Ragged Industrial School', one of his many schemes for improving the lot of the city's poor. At the corner of Ramsay Lane and Castlehill stands the Outlook Tower (I). Its four lower floors date from the seventeenth century, when it was the town house of the Lairds of Cockpen. In the 1850s the building was taken over by an optician named Maria Theresa Short, who added an octagonal three-storey tower and installed a Camera Obscura in the topmost storey: 'Short's Observatory', as it came to be known, turned out to be one of the great attractions of the day. It was largely the possibilities of development which this suggested that prompted Patrick Geddes to take over the whole building in 1892 and convert the Tower into what he called 'The World's First Sociological Laboratory', with a variety of exhibitions designed to stress man's interrelationship with his environment. As with Geddes' residential ventures, it soon became necessary to establish a company to run the building, and the Outlook Tower Association was formed to develop his ideas. This did not prove entirely successful, and in 1940 the building was taken over by Castlehill Properties, whose intention was to create in it a memorial to Patrick Geddes. Again little was done, and when the University of Edinburgh acquired control of the property in 1964 much of the interior was derelict. The Camera Obscura continued to be operated as a tourist attraction, often manned during the summer by University students, but the University's intention of using the rest of the building as exhibition space for its Department of Urban Design and Regional Planning (a project that would surely have had Geddes' blessing) has not been able to be realised. In 1977 the Outlook Tower was leased, and then later sold, to Visitor Centres Ltd., who continue to run the Camera Obscura and are developing more of the lower floors for tourist purposes.

Castlehill

When Mylne's open courtyards were still a new and untried concept, even their most sceptical opponent might have been convinced of their good qualities had he but taken the trouble to compare Mylne's Court with what lay immediately to the west. In the stretch of Castlehill between Mylne's Court and the Outlook Tower were no fewer than five closes, Blyth's, Nairn's, Tod's, Jollie's, and Sempill's, each giving access to a crowded and haphazard collection of dwelling houses. Most of this property was demolished in the 1840s, to be replaced by the Assembly Hall of the Free Church, opened in 1859. Amongst the buildings which disappeared at this time was the house of Mary of Guise, mentioned in chapter 3. It was a substantial dwelling running parallel to Castlehill but hidden from it by the tenements which fronted the street; access to it was by Tod's, Nairn's, and Blyth's closes. The point should be made that the royal residence is not to be confused either with Somerville's Land (an error into which even those notable authorities, Macgibbon and Ross, have fallen in their *Castellated and Domestic Architecture of Scotland*) or with Sempill's Lodging (see below), whose turnpike stair is sometimes wrongly claimed to be the only surviving portion of Mary's mansion.

A further group of dilapidated buildings between Sempill's Close and the Outlook Tower was cleared before 1900 to provide adequate access to the new kitchen of the Rainy Hall, and the resulting kitchen yard (e) remains the only gap site in the upper part of the Royal Mile. Suggestions are made periodically that the gap should be filled: while it would be possible to erect a 'bridge' building at first floor level to link the Outlook Tower with Sempill's Close and still leave ready access to the kitchen, the cost of such a scheme has so far rendered it impracticable. The yard has in recent years served as a convenient 'backstage' area for the organisers of the Military Tattoo on the Castle Esplanade during the period of the Edinburgh Festival. Not only is it a handy parking space for vehicles and equipment, but it has also been a useful temporary 'stable' for animals performing in the Tattoo while they await their turn on the Esplanade: horses in 1973 and again in 1978, Rebecca the baby elephant in 1974, and a colourful assortment of regimental mascots in 1977 — a goat, a ram, an Irish wolfhound, and a Shetland pony.

The only group of old buildings remaining in this whole area is that consisting of Sempill's House (J), which now closes off the foot of Sempill's Close (f), and the two sections of the building lying between Sempill's Close and Jollie's Close, property that is now known, somewhat illogically, simply as 'Sempill's Close' (K). Before the building of Moncrieff Hall effectively cut it off, the actual close skirted Sempill's House and continued northwards as far as Mound Place, where it emerged through the pend that is now the entrance to Patrick Geddes Hall. The archway of the close may still be seen at second floor level on the back wall of the house known as 'Sempill's Close'.

Two of the doorways of Sempill's House have lintels bearing the date 1638, together with inscriptions and armorial bearings, which are said to resemble those of the Craig family but have not been conclusively identified. Immediately prior to 1743, this property consisted of two dwelling houses, the lower one ("a hall, two chambers, a kitchen and study, garret and cellar")[70] belonging to David Brown, merchant, and the upper one ("a hall, kitchen, chamber, cellar, and loft") belonging to Patrick Manderston, merchant. In 1743, they sold their houses to Hugh, twelfth Lord Sempill, who created "a great lodging or dwelling-house, consisting of a kitchen or two large rooms in the first storey, four rooms in the second storey, and four rooms in the top or garret storey, with two cellars". The property passed from Hugh, who commanded Cumberland's left wing at Culloden, to his son John, the thirteenth Lord, who sold it in 1755 to Sir John Clerk of Penicuik. He in turn disposed of it in 1760 to a Mr Williamson of Foxhall, and it appears to have had a variety of owners thereafter: the Sempill name, however, has remained, despite the family's short association with the building.

When the Rainy Hall was built, the two lower floors of the house were converted into ancillary accommodation for the kitchen, and when this was extended in the 1960s further alterations were made, one storey now being used as a tank room. At some period, presumably when the Rainy Hall kitchen was first constructed, the top floor of Sempill's House was removed, no doubt because of increasing dilapidation, but the roof-top features were carefully redesigned and the building does not give the impression of having been decapitated.

The building now known as Sempill's Close is entered from the old Jollie's Close (g) at 537 Castlehill. Its inner part, consisting of three floors and an attic, appears to have been built around the same time as Sempill's House and is an excellent example of vernacular building of the period, typical of the kind of dwelling which at one time filled the whole north side of Castlehill. Its small rooms had the customary decorative plaster cornices with wood panelling and moulded skirtings; there is a well-preserved turnpike stair, and a roof-line that is particularly appealing, seen to best advantage from the upper storeys of Mylne's Court. Joined to this, and fronting Castlehill, is a somewhat undistinguished piece of mid-nineteenth-century work, with a shop on the ground floor and two storeys above. The earlier building which this replaced was apparently of much greater character, a two-storey dwelling belonging originally to "the chaplain of the chaplainry of St Nicholas' Altar",[71] an ecclesiastical foundation associated with St Giles.

Little is known of the history of these buildings prior to their acquisition by the University of Edinburgh in 1966. By this time they were unoccupied, and rapidly approaching a state of dereliction, so rapidly that in 1968 the more important surviving pieces of original timber panelling were removed to safe keeping to prevent their further deterioration. The subsequent renovation of Mylne's Court and Patrick Geddes Hall left Sempill's Close as the only piece of University property in the Mound/Lawnmarket area still to be restored, and it was imperative that it too should be rehabilitated, both for its own sake and in order to complete the conservation of an important corner of the Old Town. By 1979, the necessary finance had been gathered together from various sources, £210,000 in all, and in October of that year work commenced on site, again under the expert direction of Ian G. Lindsay and Partners.

The front block was in relatively good condition, and each floor has been converted into a two-person flat with comparatively little alteration to the existing fabric, apart from the addition of bathroom and kitchen facilities: the shop on the ground floor has been retained. The much older inner part, however, was very dilapidated, both inside and out, and the only procedure that could be adopted was to gut this part of the building completely, refurbish the exterior by renewing the roof and carrying out major repairs to the walls, and then reinstate the interior. Each of the three floors is now a four-person flat: the original layout of rooms has been retained as far as possible, the salvaged panelling has been restored in two of the rooms and the new interior finishes have been carefully matched with such original features as survived. Early in 1981 Sempill's Close was re-occupied, its sixteen students living in modernised flats that nonetheless retain an atmosphere of a much earlier period; their completion signalled the end of the University's arduous and costly, but immensely successful, programme of conservation in the Mound/Lawnmarket area.

While the principal credit for this recent programme of conservation and improvement must go to the University of Edinburgh, it is surely possible to trace throughout the guiding

10 Mylne's Court from the roof of the Outlook Tower.

11 The 'painted' room, Edward Salvesen Hall (see p. 29).

12 The Mound from the roof of the Royal Institution, 1844. The north block of Mylne's Court is to the left of the steeple of the Tolbooth Kirk. In front of Mylne's Court are the offices of *The Edinburgh Observer* and to their right lies Fox Hall. The substantial building further to the right is what is now Patrick Geddes Hall (see p. 76).

13   The Mound today. New College has replaced Fox Hall, and the roof-tops of Mylne's Court can just be seen to the left of its two central.

hand of Patrick Geddes, whose hopes for the "renaissance of historic Edinburgh" have in this area at least been fulfilled. Perhaps it is even possible behind him to trace dimly through the centuries the influence of that early master of improvement, Robert Mylne. The process which started with his "great, square building" in the Lawnmarket still continues, and the result is precisely what he hoped for: "the decorment of the good Town" and "the great convenience and accommodation" of its citizens.

EPILOGUE

"A MÊLÉE OF HETEROGENEOUS SPIRITS":
student life

Patrick Geddes' seven students of 1887 were the pioneers of a movement that has grown enormously. His University Hall began as a very modest institution, and even its staunchest supporters could not have foreseen the extent to which the ideas it embodied were to develop throughout the next eighty years. In Edinburgh, residential accommodation provided and run by the University developed along three separate lines. Muir Hall, Masson Hall, Cowan House, and New College Residence have already been mentioned, individual halls of medium size and traditional organisation, accommodating between thirty and eighty students each. In the early 1960s a number of smaller properties throughout Edinburgh were acquired by the University and converted into Student Houses, most of them providing accommodation for upwards of ten students, who cooked their own meals in a communal kitchen. Most significantly, a major step forward was taken in the late 1950s with the planning of the Pollock Halls of Residence, a massive complex including nine modern halls and two Scots baronial-style mansions in an attractive setting under the slopes of Arthur's Seat; opened between 1960 and 1973, the Pollock Halls form the University's largest residential unit, housing over 1800 students.

To these three quite separate categories of accommodation Mylne's Court was added in the late 1960s. It was a valuable addition, not just in increasing the number of rooms available — and with a total student population in the University of over 11,000 even a comparatively small increase was welcome — but in further diversifying the types of accommodation on offer. Student Houses were developed with the more independent resident in mind, and were initially not available to first-year students. The

103

Pollock Halls provided the largest number of student places, but such a complex, however hard it tries to resist the tendency — and the Pollock Halls have tried hard, and generally successfully — can in one sense never be anything other than an institution: the sheer size of it is an unavoidable constraint, as is the uniformity imposed by modern buildings and limited budgets. Muir and Masson Halls offered an alternative for female students, smaller traditional establishments with an independent outlook and a more intimate character; New College Residence did the same for male divinity students, but after the closure of Cowan House in 1964 there was no comparable residence for male students in general. This was the gap which Edward Salvesen Hall was designed to fill. Another gap which had long been recognised in the University's residential provisions was in the postgraduate area: the great increase in postgraduate numbers in the post-war years had on several occasions prompted the suggestion that a specifically postgraduate hall be built, but pressure was even greater in the undergraduate sector and the dream of a postgraduate hall was not to be realised until Philip Henman Hall was designated as such.

The restoration of Mylne's Court was thus significant on much more than mere historical and architectural grounds. Its use as a hall of residence was not, of course, without drawbacks. As a listed building, its exterior could not be altered: the internal layout was therefore governed by the position of the existing windows, and because it also had to conform to government regulations which stipulated maximum and minimum sizes for students' rooms, there is a preponderance of double rooms. It is too small to provide as flexible a meals service as is possible in a larger establishment. Its smallness also prevents it from enjoying the economies of scale available to bigger institutions, and it is in general less economic to run. These drawbacks are more than countered by the advantages of life in Mylne's Court. Nowhere else in Edinburgh does this particular brand of student accommodation exist: a place with an undefinable atmosphere, a building of considerable character in which almost every room has its own separate identity, a community small enough for most people to get to know each other and yet not so small that it suffers the unnatural stresses and pressures to which certain kinds of community units are prone — and all this in Edinburgh's Royal Mile, one minute's walk from the

Castle, ideally located for most areas of the University, for transport within and outside the city, for shops, theatres, restaurants, discos, and all the other attractions of a capital city: small wonder that the vast majority of students who come to live here become thirled to the place.

As mentioned above, Edward Salvesen Hall was first occupied by male undergraduates, 102 in all, in 42 single and 30 double study-bedrooms. In 1981 the hall became mixed, and a new era began. When Patrick Geddes Hall joined Mylne's Court in 1978, it provided a further 77 places, in 17 single and 30 double study-bedrooms, for both male and female undergraduates. The undergraduates in these halls are for the most part British: an average of 60-70% come from Scotland, 20% from England, and the rest from overseas, perhaps on one of the official exchange programmes which the University operates with Pennsylvania or Tübingen, or perhaps simply because Edinburgh has an international reputation in their chosen field of study. All Faculties of the University are generally represented: Science accounts for an annual average of 30-40%, Arts, Social Science, and Divinity 10-15% each (the proportion of Divinity students is high, as a result of the historical connection with New College), while Law, Medicine, Music, and Veterinary Medicine share the remainder.

Philip Henman Hall can accommodate 74 postgraduates, 57 of these in three-person flats, each of which includes a fully equipped kitchen, and the remainder in 6 double and 5 single study-bedrooms; among this number are usually four or five married couples. The most striking feature of the hall is its unashamedly international composition. In the six years from 1973 to 1979 the 405 residents came from no fewer than 67 different countries: if one excludes the 77 students from the four 'home' countries of the United Kingdom and the 55 Americans (the largest single national group), the remaining 273 students represented 62 different nationalities. Or, to look at the statistics in a different way, in any given term there were never fewer than 26 different nationalities among the residents, normally there were over 30, and in one term there were 34. There can be few other establishments, let alone other University Halls of Residence, where over 30 nationalities live together under one roof — and it has to be remembered that in the context of Philip Henman Hall, with its double rooms and its three-person flats, 'living together' means not just reading newspapers in the same common room or watching the same television programme: it can, and often does, mean three people of vastly dissimilar social and cultural backgrounds — a sophisticated West coast American, perhaps, an Arab girl not quite used to the emancipation of the western world, and one of the colourful and fun-loving people of the East, from Thailand or Singapore or Japan — three people who have never met before and who may at the start of the year have very little in common, running a flat together, cooking meals together, two of them sharing a bedroom. Problems and disagreements there are, of course, but the wonder of it is that on the whole the system works. All parts of the globe are represented, and all branches of learning: the town-planner from Mexico, the business expert from Indonesia, theologians from Hungary and Korea, linguists from Thailand and Algeria, the Nigerian agriculturalist and the Zambian politician, the vets from Cyprus and Burma, the social workers from Ireland, the civil engineer from Nepal ... the list is endless, and the assortment is fascinating. International dinner parties, with each resident providing a sample of one of his or her national dishes, are a particular delight. World-wide friendships are created that have continued after the flatmates have returned to their separate continents, and not a few inter-continental marriages owe their beginnings to residence in Philip Henman Hall. One can, of course, make too much of this, but many of these overseas postgraduates are sponsored by their governments or their home Universities and return to influential positions in their own countries: is it naïve to feel that in providing them with a comfortable and friendly atmosphere in which for a year they may share their lives with colleagues from other nations, Mylne's Court is playing its part in promoting good international relations?

To look after this large and diverse student population, a staff of over 40 people is required: cooks, kitchen assistants, boilermen, cleaners, servitors. These are supervised by a Domestic Bursar and an Assistant Domestic Bursar, who are responsible for financial and factorial matters and are in charge of the domestic management of the halls, including the Rainy Hall kitchen. A Warden and three Assistant Wardens share the day-to-day running of Mylne's Court with them: they deal with all business relating to the student residents, and the Warden is responsible overall for the general conduct, organisation, and discipline of the halls.

These members of staff are, of course, involved in the running of the halls all year round, and not merely during the thirty weeks of term. From earliest times, it has been a tradition in halls of residence to utilise their empty accommodation during the University vacations: University Hall in its first summer in 1887 hosted what were called 'Summer Science Courses' for interested members of the public. These were the forerunners of the summer schools and other courses which provide Mylne's Court with a large proportion of its vacation business today: academic conferences sponsored by various University departments, British Council seminars, and independently run courses of one kind or another. On occasions, groups of artists appearing in Festival productions have booked accommodation in Mylne's Court; so, too, have parties of Festival-goers. Latterly, in common with many other halls throughout Britain who operate through the British Universities' Accommodation Consortium, Mylne's Court has also acted virtually as a hotel, taking in casual visitors for one-night stays or for longer periods of holiday. For a number of years, too, the common room in Edward Salvesen Hall provided an attractive setting for an exhibition of paintings held as part of the Festival Fringe. All these vacation activities have two quite distinct purposes: they add considerably to the facilities which Edinburgh is able to offer to the visitor, be he tourist, summer student, or conference participant, and they earn money for the University's accommodation budget, thus helping to keep term-time rents at a more manageable level than they would otherwise be.

The importance of these summer activities is therefore not to be underestimated, but they must not be allowed to obscure the fact that the halls are for students and that it is the student life of a hall which is the core of its existence. Student life, of course, is very much the same from one place to another, and this is not the place to chronicle the multifarious manifestations of it which may be observed within Mylne's Court. The organisation of the 'official' social events — and indeed the organisation of much more than the social events — has been carried out by a series of efficient House Committees, ably chaired by student Presidents: termly dances, a revue, the annual Burns Supper, and even the Mylne's Court

Haggis Hunt, instituted in 1975 as part of a build-up to a Burns Night to be attended by a large number of overseas residents, and continued for a few years thereafter as an annual expedition to the various known haunts of the wild haggis around Edinburgh in the hope of catching sufficient tasty specimens for the following day's feast. Edward Salvesen Hall has provided the University with an editor for its student newspaper and a winner for its 'Mastermind' competition. Football teams flourish, only to fade again; a proposed hockey team did not even reach the stage of flourishing; table-tennis and darts competitions are keenly fought. Mylne's Court can claim no credit for the individual sportsmen in its midst, but it is worth recording that in 1978 almost 20% of the sporting Blues awarded by the University to men went to students who had lived there: nor is it every hall that can claim an international croquet player among its residents. On a more light-hearted level, many are the incidents that spring to mind: the activities of 'The Mylnditz Escape Committee', or the weekend when the doors to all the showers mysteriously disappeared, or the night one smooth young lawyer returned from a dinner party to find his bed solemnly reposing in the courtyard, the covers neatly turned down and his slippers in their proper place, or the occasion when the room of one of the hall's most noteworthy characters was completely filled to waist height with crumpled pieces of newspaper ... and no doubt many other such occurrences that never reach a Warden's ears. Student life, of course, is not all play, and a surprising amount of work manages to get done in the odd moments between one practical joke and the next: distinguished theses have come out of Philip Henman Hall, and a succession of good undergraduate degrees has been recorded.

On all counts, then, the students for whom Mylne's Court provides a home live life to the full — and to give an opportunity for this is, after all, the whole point of a hall of residence. In doing so, they have brought life back to this historic courtyard, life of a different quality and of a kind that it did not know before. Robert Mylne, one feels, would have approved.

GLOSSARY

Appended here are brief notes on some terms used in the text peculiar to Scottish society and institutions, which may be unfamiliar to non-Scottish readers.

Advocate: A member of the Scottish Bar with the right to appear and plead in the superior courts. The *Faculty of Advocates*, the body which comprises such people, dates from the early sixteenth century. The *Lord Advocate* is the head of the system of public prosecution in the criminal courts.

Bailie: The magistrate officiating in the burgh court and elected by the Town Council from amongst their number.

Bow: An arched gateway in a street.

Burgh: 'Burgh' is the accepted form in Scotland of the English 'borough', i.e. a market town whose inhabitants had trading privileges. Edinburgh is one of the earliest burghs known in Scotland, and was a royal burgh, i.e. one on royal lands, by c. 1125. The formerly separate burgh of Canongate became dependent on the city of Edinburgh in 1639 and was finally absorbed in 1856.

Close: A narrow passageway off a street.

Commissioner of Supply: An official who was in charge of the assessment of land tax, and who had a wide variety of other administrative duties in Scottish counties.

Committee of Estates: During the years 1640–51 the Scottish Parliament appointed this committee to act on its behalf; it included individuals who were not members of Parliament.

Court of Session: The supreme civil court in Scotland, presided over by the *Lords of Council and Session*, otherwise known as *Senators of the College of Justice*, and headed by the *Lord President*. The Court buildings are situated in Parliament Square, to the south of St Giles.

Deacon: The elected head of a *craft guild*, the body regulating the activities of a particular craft or trade.

Dean of Guild: The head of the merchant guild of a burgh. His court originally dealt with mercantile and trading affairs, but was later restricted to the supervision of building operations.

General Assembly: The highest court of the Church of Scotland, presided over by the *Moderator*.

Laird: The proprietor of a landed estate.

Land: A group of dwellings built above each other under one roof and having a common entry, occasionally with an external stair.

Lord Clerk Register: The official in charge of the administration of the royal Scottish archives.

Lyon King of Arms: The Lord Lyon has supreme jurisdiction in Scotland over armorial matters, and maintains the record of grants of arms in the *Lyon Register*. His heralds and other officials are collectively known as the *Lyon Court*.

Notary Public: A lawyer authorised to authenticate and record legal transactions.

Pend: A passage leading under a building to a courtyard.

Port: The entrance or gateway of a burgh.

Presbytery: A court of the Church of Scotland, with jurisdiction over a particular geographical area.

Provost: The principal official of a burgh, generally elected by the community.

Sheriff: The chief judge of a Scottish county.

Tenement: A building divided into several dwellings; a synonym for *land*.

Tolbooth: The meeting place of the burgh court, usually incorporating a prison. Edinburgh's Tolbooth stood just to the west of St Giles, and when the city parishes were reorganised in 1641 one of the two new parishes created took its name from this building. The congregation worshipped within St Giles until the Tolbooth Kirk was built in 1840-3.

Tron: A weigh-beam (e.g. for butter or salt) in the burgh marketplace. One of Edinburgh's new parishes of 1641 took its name from this, and the place of worship, the new church called Christ's Kirk at the Tron, is frequently referred to as the Tron Kirk.

Writer to the Signet: A solicitor or lawyer operating in Scotland before the *Court of Session*. 'Writer' is an old word for 'solicitor' in Scotland.

Wynd: A narrow street.

REFERENCES

1 J. W. Watson in *The Third Statistical Account of Scotland, vol. xv: Edinburgh* (Glasgow 1966), 17
2 Document signed by Robert Mylne, quoted in I. A. Stirling, *Mylne Square*, Book of the Old Edinburgh Club 14 (Edinburgh 1925), 46
3 *ibid.*
4 Unless separately acknowledged, quotations in chapter 2 derive from R. S. Mylne, *The Master Masons to the Crown of Scotland* (Edinburgh 1893)
5 *Acts of the Parliaments of Scotland*, 11, 1424-1567 (London 1814), 335
6 M. Wood, ed., *Extracts from the Records of the Burgh of Edinburgh 1655-1665* (Edinburgh 1940), 249-50 [22 July 1661]
7 From an undated manuscript preserved by descendants of Robert Mylne inside a framed copy of his arms, and presented to Mylne's Court in 1970
8 All quotations in this paragraph derive from *Inventory of the Writs and Evidents of the several Old Tenements of Land ... Disponed ... to Robert Miln*, Moses Bundles (supp. 4/120), Edinburgh City Archives
9 E. W. M. Balfour-Melville, ed., *The Register of the Privy Council of Scotland*, third series, 15, 1690 (Edinburgh 1967), 348
10 H. Armet, ed., *Extracts from the Records of the Burgh of Edinburgh 1689-1701* (Edinburgh 1962), 285 [13 August 1701]
11 H. Armet, ed., *Extracts from the Records of the Burgh of Edinburgh 1701-1718* (Edinburgh 1967), 43 [31 March 1703]
12 *Registration of Factory by Thomas Moffat in favour of George Watson*, Register of Deeds: Durie Office, vol. 87, 852
13 *Inventory of the Writs ...*, Moses Bundles (supp. 4/120), Edinburgh City Archives
14 T. Craufurd, *History of the University of Edinburgh 1580-1646* (Edinburgh 1808), 136
15 M. Wood, ed., *Extracts from the Records of the Burgh of Edinburgh 1626-1641* (Edinburgh 1936), 224 [17 December 1639]
16 *Churches (Scotland) Act Commission, Order no. 661* (1909), 10
17 Quotations on pages 31 to 33 derive from M. Wood, ed., *Edinburgh Poll Tax Returns 1694*, Scottish Record Society (1951)
18 H. Armet, ed., *Extracts from the Records of the Burgh of Edinburgh 1689-1701* (Edinburgh 1962), 66 [20 May 1691]
19 British Library Lansdown MS 605 f.54a
20 H. Armet, ed., *Extracts from the Records of the Burgh of Edinburgh 1701-1718* (Edinburgh 1967), 287 [13 May 1715]
21 *ibid.*, 353 [21 May 1718]
22 Letter from McLurgg to Russell, 23 August 1687, Russell MSS 308/2, Scottish Record Office
23 Journal of Patrick MacDowall, quoted in J. Prebble, *The Darien Disaster* (Edinburgh 1968), 305

24 Unattributed quotation in Prebble, *The Darien Disaster*, 310

25 W. Ferguson, *Scotland: 1689 to the Present* (Edinburgh 1968), 116

26 H. Scott, *Fasti Ecclesiae Scoticanae*, vol. 1 (Edinburgh 1915), 123

27 *ibid.*, 120

28 Sir D. Wilson, *Memorials of Edinburgh in the Olden Time* (2nd edition, Edinburgh 1891), I, 182

29 F. A. Pottle and C. H. Bennett, edd., *Boswell's Journal of a Tour to the Hebrides with Samuel Johnson, 1773* (London 1963), 32 [17 August 1773]

30 The remaining quotations in chapter 4 derive from *Register of Testaments, Edinburgh Commissariat*, Scottish Record Office

31 J. Grant, *Old and New Edinburgh* (London 1880-3), I, 122

32 Sir John Lauder of Fountainhall, ed., *The Decisions of the Lords of Council and Session 1678-1712* (Edinburgh 1761), 551-2

33 Private communication

34 Moses Bundles 166/6436, Edinburgh City Archives

35 Letter from the Misses Jane and Mary Grant to Lady Grant of Rothiemurchus, 22 August 1822, quoted in B. Skinner, ed., *A Contemporary Account of the Royal Visit to Edinburgh, 1822*, Book of the Old Edinburgh Club 31 (Edinburgh 1962), 129-30

36 J. H. Jamieson, *The Sedan Chair in Edinburgh*, Book of the Old Edinburgh Club 9 (Edinburgh 1916), 228

37 Grant, *Old and New Edinburgh*, I, 90

38 D. Wilson, *Memorials of Edinburgh in the Olden Time* (Edinburgh 1848), I, 159

39 *The Biographical Dictionary of the Society for the Diffusion of Useful Knowledge*, vol. II (London 1843), 590

40 R. Mein, *City Cleaned and Country Improven* (Edinburgh 1760), foreword

41 F. A. Pottle and C. H. Bennett, edd., *Boswell's Journal*, 11 [14 August 1773]

42 *Proposals for carrying on certain Public Works in the City of Edinburgh* (Edinburgh 1752), 7-8

43 W. M. Gilbert, *Edinburgh in the Nineteenth Century* (Edinburgh 1901), 78ff.

44 *The Scotsman*, 20 April 1825

45 H. Johnston, *Letter to the Lord Provost, Magistrates, and Council of the City of Edinburgh on the State of the Closes in the Lawnmarket, High Street, Canongate, and Cowgate* (Edinburgh 1856), 23

46 *1871 Census of Scotland: Edinburgh*, Registrar General for Scotland, New Register House

47 C. Ryskamp and F. A. Pottle, edd., *Boswell: The Ominous Years, 1774-1776* (London 1963), 231

48 Appendix to *Memorandum* submitted by the Free Church to the Churches (Scotland) Act Commission, April 1905

49 *Reports to the General Assembly of the Church of Scotland 1960* (Edinburgh 1960), 805

50 *ibid.* (1961), 866

51 Committee of Vice-Chancellors and Principals, *The Planning of University Halls of Residence* (Oxford 1948), 10ff.

52 P. Boardman, *Patrick Geddes, Maker of the Future* (Chapel Hill 1944), 104

53 *The Cheilead*, no. vi (November 1826), 70

54 Unattributed quotation in A. J. Youngson, *The Making of Classical Edinburgh* (Edinburgh 1966), 280

55 P. Geddes, *University Studies and University Residence* in Geddes et al., *Halls of Residence for University Students* (Edinburgh 1906), 21

56 *Edinburgh University Calendar 1910-1911*, 803

57 *Report of University Hall 1890-1891*, quoted in Boardman, *Patrick Geddes, Maker of the Future*, 149

58 Geddes Papers 12/10/a, University of Strathclyde Archives

59 Unattributed quotation in Boardman, *Patrick Geddes, Maker of the Future*, 151

60 Reported by Arthur Geddes in a *Note on University Hall*, Geddes Papers 12/10/a, University of Strathclyde Archives

61 *Edinburgh University Calendar 1894-1895*, app. 15

62 Letter from nine past residents "about the financial crisis threatening to jeopardize the future of University Hall", 6 June 1912, National Library of Scotland (shelf no. 6.2376)

63 *Edinburgh University Calendar 1888-1889*, app. 18

64 Quoted in P. Boardman, *The Worlds of Patrick Geddes* (London 1978), 431

65 P. Geddes et al., *Interpretation of the Paintings in the Common Room of Ramsay Lodge* (Edinburgh n.d.)

66 Letter from Principal Baillie to Lord Kilmaine, Secretary of the Pilgrim Trust, July 1953, New College archives

67 *Reports to the General Assembly of the Church of Scotland 1961* (Edinburgh 1961), 867

68 Quoted in University of Edinburgh, *Mound/Lawnmarket: an area for conservation* (Edinburgh 1970), 19

69 *The Planning of University Halls of Residence*, 23

70 *Churches (Scotland) Act Commission, Order no. 22* (1909), 21-2

71 Title deeds of building, quoted in D. Wilson, *Reminiscences of Old Edinburgh* (Edinburgh 1878), I, 119